24/7

Jonathan Crary is Meyer Schapiro Professor of Modern Art and Theory at Columbia University. His books include *Techniques of the Observer, Suspensions of Perception, Scorched Earth*, and *Tricks of the Light*.

24/7

Late Capitalism and the Ends of Sleep

Jonathan Crary

VERSO

London • New York

This edition first published by Verso 2025
First published by Verso 2013
© Jonathan Crary 2013

The manufacturer's authorized representative in the EU for product safety
(GPSR) is LOGOS EUROPE, 9 rue Nicolas Poussin, 17000, La Rochelle, France
contact@logoseurope.eu

1 3 5 7 9 10 8 6 4 2

Verso
UK: 6 Meard Street, London W1F 0EG
US: 207 East 32nd Street, New York, NY 10016
versobooks.com

Verso is the imprint of New Left Books

ISBN-13: 978-1-80429-840-4
eISBN-13: 978-1-78168-311-8 (US)
eISBN-13: 978-1-78168-476-4 (UK)

British Library Cataloguing in Publication Data
A catalogue record for this book is available from the British Library

The Library of Congress Has Cataloged the Hardback Edition as Follows:

Crary, Jonathan.
  24/7 : terminal capitalism and the ends of sleep / Jonathan Crary.
    pages cm
  ISBN 978-1-78168-093-3 (hardback)
  1. Art and society. 2. Time and art. 3. Capitalism—Social aspects. 4. Civilization,
  Modern—21st century. I. Title. II. Title: Twenty-four seven.
  N72.S6C733 2013
  304.2'37—dc23

                                                    2013005056

Typeset in Electra by MJ Gavan, Truro, Cornwall
Printed and bound by CPI Group (UK) Ltd, Croydon CR0 4YY

for Suzanne

Or else we make a scarecrow of the day,
Loose ends and jumble of our common world

W. H. Auden

ACKNOWLEDGEMENTS

I am especially grateful to Sebastian Budgen for his support of this project and for his valuable suggestions during its completion.

The opportunity to test out parts of this work in lecture form was enormously helpful to me. I would like to thank Jorge Ribalta, Carles Guerra, and the Barcelona Museum of Contemporary Art for providing me with the venue where I first presented some of this book's content. I'm also grateful to Ron Clark and the participants in the Whitney Museum Independent Study Program for their challenging responses to my seminars. Others who generously extended speaking invitations include Hal Foster, Stefan Andriopoulos, Brian Larkin, Lorenz Engell, Bernhard Siegert, Anne Bonney, David Levi Strauss, and Serge Guilbaut and the Fine Arts students at the University of British Columbia.

Thanks also for help of many kinds to Stephanie O'Rourke,

Jonathan Crary

Siddhartha Lokanandi, Alice Attie, Kent Jones, Molly Nesbit, Harold Veeser, Chia-Ling Lee, Jesper Olsson, Cecilia Grönberg, and the late Lewis Cole. I'm indebted to my sons Chris and Owen for all they have taught me. This book is for my wife Suzanne.

24/17

CHAPTER ONE

Anyone who has lived along the west coast of North America may well know that, each year, hundreds of species of birds migrate seasonally up and down for various distances along that continental shelf. One of these species is the white-crowned sparrow. Their route in the fall takes them from Alaska to northern Mexico and then back north again every spring. Unlike most other birds, this type of sparrow has a highly unusual capacity for staying awake, for as long as seven days during migrations. This seasonal behavior enables them to fly and navigate by night and forage for nourishment by day without rest. Over the past five years the US Defense Department has spent large amounts of money to study these creatures. Researchers with government funding at various universities, notably in Madison, Wisconsin, have been investigating the brain activity of the birds during these long sleepless periods, with the hope of acquiring knowledge applicable to human beings. The aim is to discover ways to enable people to go without sleep *and* to function productively and efficiently. The initial objective, quite simply, is the creation of the sleepless soldier, and the white-crowned sparrow study project is only one small part of a broader military effort to achieve at least limited mastery over human sleep. Initiated by the advanced research division of the Pentagon (DARPA),[1] scientists in various labs are conducting experimental trials of sleeplessness techniques, including neurochemicals, gene therapy, and transcranial magnetic stimulation. The near-term goal is the development of methods to allow a combatant to go for a minimum of seven days without sleep, and in the longer term perhaps at least double that time frame, while preserving high levels of mental and physical performance. Existing means of producing sleeplessness have always been accompanied by deleterious cognitive and psychic deficits (for example, reduced alertness). This was the case with the widespread use of amphetamines in most twentieth-century wars, and more recently with drugs like Provigil. The scientific quest here is not to find ways of stimulating wakefulness but rather to reduce the body's *need* for sleep.

For over two decades, the strategic logic of US military planning has been directed toward removing the living individual from many parts of the command, control, and execution circuit. Untold billions are spent developing robotic and other remote-operated targeting and killing systems, with results that have been dismayingly evident in Pakistan, Afghanistan, and elsewhere. However, despite the extravagant claims made for new weaponry paradigms and the constant references by military analysts to the human agent as the anomalous "bottleneck" in advanced systems operations, the military's need for large human armies is not going to diminish in any foreseeable future. The sleeplessness research should be understood as one part of a quest for soldiers whose physical capabilities will more closely approximate the functionalities of non-human apparatuses and networks. There are massive ongoing efforts by the scientific-military complex to develop forms of "augmented cognition" that will enhance many kinds of human-machine interaction. Simultaneously, the military is also funding many other areas of brain research, including the development of an anti-fear drug. There will be occasions when, for example, missile-armed drones cannot be used and death squads of sleep-resistant, fear-proofed commandos will be needed for missions of indefinite duration. As part of these endeavors, white-crowned sparrows have been removed from the seasonal rhythms of the Pacific coast environment to aid in the imposition of a machinic model of duration and efficiency onto the human body. As history has shown, war-related innovations are inevitably assimilated into a broader social sphere, and the sleepless soldier would be the forerunner of the sleepless worker or consumer. Non-sleep products, when aggressively promoted by pharmaceutical companies, would become first a lifestyle option, and eventually, for many, a necessity.

24/7 markets and a global infrastructure for continuous work and consumption have been in place for some time, but now a human subject is in the making to coincide with these more intensively.

In the late 1990s a Russian/European space consortium announced plans to build and launch into orbit satellites that would reflect sunlight back onto earth. The scheme called for a chain of many satellites to be placed in sun-synchronized orbits at an altitude of 1700 kilometers, each one equipped with fold-out parabolic reflectors of paper-thin material. Once fully extended to 200 meters in diameter, each mirror satellite would have the capacity to illuminate a ten-square-mile area on earth with a brightness nearly 100 times greater than moonlight. The initial impetus for the project was to provide illumination for industrial and natural resource exploitation in remote geographical areas with long polar nights in Siberia and western Russia, allowing outdoor work to proceed round the clock. But the company subsequently expanded its plans to include the possibility of supplying nighttime lighting for entire metropolitan areas. Reasoning that it could reduce energy costs for electric lighting, the company's slogan pitched its services as "daylight all night long." Opposition to the project arose immediately and from many directions. Astronomers expressed dismay because of the consequences for most earth-based space observation. Scientists and environmentalists declared it would have detrimental physiological consequences for both animals and humans, in that the absence of regular alternations between night and day would disrupt various metabolic patterns, including sleep. There

4

were also protests from cultural and humanitarian groups, who argued that the night sky is a commons to which all of humanity is entitled to have access, and that the ability to experience the darkness of night and observe the stars is a basic human right that no corporation can nullify. However, if this is in any sense a right or privilege, it is already being violated for over half of the world's population in cities that are enveloped continuously in a penumbra of smog and high-intensity illumination. Defenders of the project, though, asserted that such technology would help lower nocturnal use of electricity, and that a loss of the night sky and its darkness is a small price to pay for reducing global energy consumption. In any case, this ultimately unworkable enterprise is one particular instance of a contemporary imaginary in which a state of permanent illumination is inseparable from the non-stop operation of global exchange and circulation. In its entrepreneurial excess, the project is a hyperbolic expression of an institutional intolerance of whatever obscures or prevents an instrumentalized and unending condition of visibility.

One of the forms of torture endured by the many victims of extrajudicial rendition, and by others imprisoned since 2001, has been the use of sleep deprivation. The facts surrounding one individual detainee have been widely noted, but his treatment was similar to the fate of hundreds of others whose cases are less well documented. Mohammed al-Qahtani was tortured according to the specifications of what is now known as the Pentagon's "First Special Interrogation Plan," authorized by

Donald Rumsfeld. Al-Qahtani was deprived of sleep for most of the time during a two-month period, when he was subjected to interrogations that often lasted twenty hours at a time. He was confined, unable to lie down, in tiny cubicles that were lit with high-intensity lamps and into which loud music was broadcast. Within the military intelligence community these prisons are referred to as Dark Sites, although one of the locations where al-Qahtani was incarcerated was code-named Camp Bright Lights. This is hardly the first time sleep deprivation has been used by Americans or their surrogates. It is misleading in some ways to single it out because, for Mohammed al-Qahtani and many others, sleep deprivation was only one part of a larger program of beatings, humiliations, prolonged restraint, and simulated drownings. Many of these "programs" for extrajudicial prisoners were custom designed by psychologists on Behavioral Science Consultation Teams to exploit what they had determined to be individual emotional and physical vulnerabilities.

Sleep deprivation as torture can be traced back many centuries, but its systematic use coincides historically with the availability of electric lighting and the means for sustained sound amplification. First practiced routinely by Stalin's police in the 1930s, sleep deprivation was usually the initial part of what the NKVD torturers called "the conveyor belt"—the organized sequences of brutalities, of useless violence that irreparably damages human beings. It produces psychosis after a relatively short period of time, and after several weeks begins to cause neurological damage. In experiments, rats will die after two to three weeks of sleeplessness. It leads to an extreme state of helplessness and compliance, in which extraction of meaningful information from the victim is impossible, in which one will confess to or fabricate anything. The denial of sleep is the violent dispossession of self by external force, the calculated shattering of an individual.

Certainly, the United States has long been involved in the practice of torture directly and through its client regimes, but notable of the post-9/11 period has been its easy relocation into the light of public visibility as merely one controversial topic among others. Numerous opinion polls show that a majority of Americans approve of torture under some circumstances. Mainstream media discussions consistently reject the assertion that sleep deprivation is torture. Rather, it is categorized as psychological persuasion, acceptable to many in the same way as is the force-feeding of hunger-striking prisoners. As Jane Mayer reported in her book *The Dark Side*, sleep deprivation was justified cynically in Pentagon documents by the fact that US Navy Seals are required to go on simulated missions without sleeping for two days.[2] It is important to note that the treatment of so-called "high-interest" prisoners at Guantánamo and elsewhere combined explicit forms of torture with complete control over sensory and perceptual experience. Inmates are required to live in windowless cells that are always lit, and they must wear eye and ear coverings that block out light and sound whenever they are escorted out of their cells to preclude any awareness of night and day, or of any stimulus that could provide cues to their whereabouts. This regime of perceptual deprivation often extends to routine daily contact between prisoners and guards, during which the latter are fully armored, gloved, and helmeted with one-way Plexiglas visors so that the prisoner is denied any visible relation to a human face, or even an inch of exposed skin. These are techniques and procedures for producing abject states of compliance, and one of the levels on which this occurs is through the fabrication of a world that radically excludes the possibility of care, protection, or solace.

This particular constellation of recent events provides a prismatic vantage point onto some of the plural consequences of neoliberal globalization and of longer processes of Western modernization. I do not intend to give this grouping any privileged explanatory significance; rather, it makes up a provisional opening onto some of the paradoxes of the expanding, non-stop life-world of twenty-first-century capitalism—paradoxes that are inseparable from shifting configurations of sleep and waking, illumination and darkness, justice and terror, and from forms of exposure, unprotectedness, and vulnerability. It might be objected that I have singled out exceptional or extreme phenomena, but if so, they are not disconnected from what have become normative trajectories and conditions elsewhere. One of those conditions can be characterized as a generalized inscription of human life into duration without breaks, defined by a principle of continuous functioning. It is a time that no longer passes, beyond clock time.

Behind the vacuity of the catchphrase, 24/7 is a static

redundancy that disavows its relation to the rhythmic and periodic textures of human life. It connotes an arbitrary, uninflected schema of a week, extracted from any unfolding of variegated or cumulative experience. To say "24/365," for example, is simply not the same, for this introduces an unwieldy suggestion of an extended temporality in which something might actually change, in which unforeseen events might happen. As I indicated initially, many institutions in the developed world have been running 24/7 for decades now. It is only recently that the elaboration, the modeling of one's personal and social identity, has been reorganized to conform to the uninterrupted operation of markets, information networks, and other systems. A 24/7 environment has the semblance of a social world, but it is actually a non-social model of machinic performance and a suspension of living that does not disclose the human cost required to sustain its effectiveness. It must be distinguished from what Lukács and others in the early twentieth century identified as the empty, homogenous time of modernity, the metric or calendar time of nations, of finance or industry, from which individual hopes or projects were excluded. What is new is the sweeping abandonment of the pretense that time is coupled to any long-term undertakings, even to fantasies of "progress" or development. An illuminated 24/7 world without shadows is the final capitalist mirage of post-history, of an exorcism of the otherness that is the motor of historical change.

24/7 is a time of indifference, against which the fragility of human life is increasingly inadequate and within which sleep has no necessity or inevitability. In relation to labor, it renders plausible, even normal, the idea of working without pause, without limits. It is aligned with what is inanimate, inert, or unageing. As an advertising exhortation it decrees the absoluteness of availability, and hence the ceaselessness of needs and their incitement, but also their perpetual non-fulfillment. The absence of restraints on consuming is not simply temporal. We are long past an era in which mainly things were accumulated. Now our bodies and identities assimilate an ever-expanding surfeit of services, images, procedures, chemicals, to a toxic and often fatal threshold. The long-term survival of the individual is always dispensable if the alternative might even indirectly admit the possibility of interludes with no shopping or its promotion. In related ways, 24/7 is inseparable from environmental catastrophe in its declaration of permanent expenditure, of endless wastefulness for its sustenance, in its terminal disruption of the cycles and seasons on which ecological integrity depends.

In its profound uselessness and intrinsic passivity, with the incalculable losses it causes in production time, circulation, and consumption, sleep will always collide with the demands of a 24/7 universe. The huge portion of our lives that we spend asleep, freed from a morass of simulated needs, subsists as one of the great human affronts to the voraciousness of contemporary capitalism. Sleep is an uncompromising interruption of the theft of time from us by capitalism. Most of the seemingly irreducible necessities of human life—hunger, thirst, sexual desire, and recently the need for friendship—have been remade into commodified or financialized forms. Sleep poses the idea of a human need and interval of time that cannot be colonized and harnessed to a massive engine of profitability, and thus remains an incongruous anomaly and site of crisis in the global present. In spite of all the scientific research in this area, it frustrates and confounds any strategies to exploit or reshape it. The stunning, inconceivable reality is that nothing of value can be extracted from it.

It should be no surprise that there is an erosion of sleep now everywhere, given the immensity of what is at stake economically. Over the course of the twentieth century there were steady inroads made against the time of sleep—the average North American adult now sleeps approximately six and a half hours a night, an erosion from eight hours a generation ago, and (hard as it is to believe) down from ten hours in the early twentieth century. In the mid twentieth century the familiar adage that "we spend a third of our lives asleep" seemed to have an axiomatic certainty, a certainty that continues to be undermined. Sleep is a ubiquitous but unseen reminder of a premodernity that has never been fully exceeded, of the agricultural universe which began vanishing 400 years ago. The scandal of sleep is the embeddedness in our lives of the rhythmic oscillations of solar light and darkness, activity and rest, of work and recuperation, that have been eradicated or neutralized elsewhere. Sleep of course has a dense history, as does anything presumed to be natural. It has never been something monolithic or identical, and over centuries and millennia it has assumed many variegated forms and patterns. In the 1930s Marcel Mauss included both sleeping and waking in his study of "Body Techniques," in which he showed that aspects of seemingly instinctive behaviors were in fact learned in an immense variety of ways through imitation or education. Nonetheless, it can still be suggested that there were crucial features common to sleep in the vast diversity of premodern agrarian societies.

By the mid seventeenth century, sleep became loosened from the stable position it had occupied in now obsolete Aristotelian and Renaissance frameworks. Its incompatibility with modern notions of productivity and rationality began to be identified, and Descartes, Hume, and Locke were only a few of the philosophers who disparaged sleep for its irrelevance to the operation of the mind or the pursuit of knowledge. It became devalued in the face of a privileging of consciousness and volition, of notions of utility, objectivity, and self-interested agency. For Locke, sleep was a regrettable if unavoidable interruption of God's intended priorities for human beings: to be industrious and rational. In the very first paragraph of Hume's *Treatise on Human Nature*, sleep is lumped together with fever and madness as examples of the obstacles to knowledge. By the mid nineteenth century, the asymmetrical relation between sleep and waking began to be conceptualized in hierarchical models in which sleep was understood as a regression to a lower and more primitive mode in which supposedly higher and more complex brain activity was inhibited. Schopenhauer is one of the rare thinkers who turned this hierarchy against itself and proposed that only in sleep could we locate "the true kernel" of human existence.

In many ways the uncertain status of sleep has to be understood in relation to the particular dynamic of modernity which

12

has invalidated any organization of reality into binary comple-
mentaries. The homogenizing force of capitalism is
incompatible with any inherent structure of differentiation:
sacred-profane, carnival-workday, nature-culture, machine-
organism, and so on. Thus any persisting notions of sleep as
somehow natural are rendered unacceptable. Of course,
people will continue to sleep, and even sprawling megacities
will still have nocturnal intervals of relative quiescence.
Nonetheless, sleep is now an experience cut loose from notions
of necessity or nature. Instead, like so much else, it is conceptualized as a variable but managed function that can only be
defined instrumentally and physiologically. Recent research
has shown that the number of people who wake themselves up
once or more at night to check their messages or data is growing exponentially. One seemingly inconsequential but
prevalent linguistic figure is the machine-based designation of
"sleep mode." The notion of an apparatus in a state of low-
power readiness remakes the larger sense of sleep into simply a
deferred or diminished condition of operationality and access.
It supersedes an off/on logic, so that nothing is ever fundamentally "off" and there is never an actual state of rest.

Sleep is an irrational and intolerable affirmation that there
might be limits to the compatibility of living beings with the
allegedly irresistible forces of modernization. One of the familiar truisms of contemporary critical thought is that there are no
unalterable givens of nature—not even death, according to
those who predict we will all soon be downloading our minds
into digital immortality. To believe that there are any essential

features that distinguish living beings from machines is, we are told by celebrated critics, naive and delusional. Why should anyone object, they would counter, if new drugs could allow someone to work at their job 100 hours straight? Would not flexible and reduced sleep time allow more personal freedom, the ability to customize one's life further in accordance with individual needs and desires? Would not less sleep allow more chance for "living life to the fullest"? But one might object that human beings are meant to sleep at night, that our own bodies are aligned with the daily rotation of our planet, and that seasonal and solar responsive behaviors occur in almost every living organism. To which the reply would likely be: pernicious New Age nonsense, or even worse, an ominous yearning for some Heideggerian connectedness to the earth. More importantly, within the globalist neoliberal paradigm, sleeping is for losers.

In the nineteenth century, following the worst abuses in the treatment of workers that accompanied industrialization in Europe, factory managers came to the realization that it would be more profitable if workers were allowed modest amounts of rest time to enable them to be more effective and sustainable producers in the long run, as Anson Rabinbach has well shown in his work on the science of fatigue. But by the last decades of the twentieth century and into the present, with the collapse of controlled or mitigated forms of capitalism in the United States and Europe, there has ceased to be any internal necessity for having rest and recuperation as components of economic growth and profitability. Time for human rest and regeneration is now simply too expensive to be structurally possible within contemporary capitalism. Teresa Brennan coined the term "bioderegulation" to describe the brutal discrepencies between the temporal operation of deregulated markets and the intrinsic physical limitations of the humans required to conform to these demands.[3]

The decline in the long-term value of living labor provides no incentive for rest or health to be economic priorities, as recent debates around healthcare have shown. There are now very few significant interludes of human existence (with the colossal exception of sleep) that have not been penetrated and taken over as work time, consumption time, or marketing time. In their analysis of contemporary capitalism, Luc Boltanski and Eve Chiapello have pointed to the array of forces that esteem the individual who is constantly engaged, interfacing, interacting, communicating, responding, or processing within some telematic milieu. In affluent regions of the globe, this has occurred, as they note, amid the dissolving of most of the borders between private and professional time, between work and consumption. In their connectionist paradigm, the highest premium is placed on activity for its own sake, "To always be doing something, to move, to change—this is what enjoys prestige, as against stability, which is often synonymous with inaction."[4] This model of activity is not some transformation of an earlier work-ethic paradigm, but is an altogether new model of normativity, and one that requires 24/7 temporalities for its realization.

To return briefly to the project mentioned earlier: the plan to launch huge orbiting reflectors as mirrors for solar light that would eliminate the darkness of nighttime has something preposterous about it, like a low-tech survival of a merely mechanical scheme from Jules Verne or early twentieth-century science fiction. In fact, the first experimental launches were essentially failures—on one occasion the reflectors did not unfold into position properly, and on another, dense cloud cover over a test city prevented a convincing demonstration of its capabilities. Its ambitions might seem related to a broad set of panoptic practices developed over the last 200 years. That is, it points back to the importance of illumination in Bentham's original model of the Panopticon, which called for flooding space with light to eliminate shadows, and to make a condition of full observability synonymous with effects of control. But for several decades other kinds of satellites have performed in far more sophisticated ways the operations of actual surveillance and accumulation of information. A modernized panopticism has expanded well beyond visible wavelengths of light to other parts of the spectrum, not to mention the many kinds of non-optical scanners and thermal and bio-sensors. The satellite project is perhaps better understood as a perpetuation of more plainly utilitarian practices initiated in the nineteenth century. Wolfgang Schivelbusch, in his history of lighting technology, shows how the broad deployment of urban street lights by the 1880s had achieved two interrelated goals: it reduced long-standing anxieties about various dangers associated with nocturnal darkness, and it expanded the time frame and thus the profitability of many economic activities.[5] The illumination of the nighttime was a symbolic demonstration of what apologists for capitalism had promised throughout the nineteenth century: it would be the twin guarantee of security and increased possibilities for prosperity, supposedly improving the fabric of social existence for everyone. In this sense, the triumphal installation of a 24/7 world is a fulfillment of that earlier project, but with benefits and prosperity accruing mainly to a powerful global elite.

24/7 steadily undermines distinctions between day and night, between light and dark, and between action and repose. It is a zone of insensibility, of amnesia, of what defeats the possibility of experience. To paraphrase Maurice Blanchot, it is both of and after the disaster, characterized by the empty sky, in which no star or sign is visible, in which one's bearings are lost and orientation is impossible.[6] More concretely, it is like a state of emergency, when a bank of floodlights are suddenly switched on in the middle of the night, seemingly as a response to some extreme circumstances, but which never get turned off and become domesticated into a permanent condition. The planet becomes reimagined as a non-stop work site or an always open shopping mall of infinite choices, tasks, selections, and digressions. Sleeplessness is the state in which producing, consuming, and discarding occur without pause, hastening the exhaustion of life and the depletion of resources.

As the major remaining obstacle—in effect, the last of what Marx called "natural barriers"—to the full realization of 24/7 capitalism, sleep cannot be eliminated. But it can be wrecked and despoiled, and, as my opening examples show, methods and motivations to accomplish this wrecking are fully in place.

The injuring of sleep is inseparable from the ongoing dismantling of social protections in other spheres. Just as universal access to clean drinking water has been programmatically devastated around the globe by pollution and privatization, with the accompanying monetization of bottled water, it is not difficult to see a similar construction of scarcity in relation to sleep. All of the encroachments on it create the insomniac conditions in which sleep must be bought (even if one is paying for a chemically modified state only approximating actual sleep). Statistics of soaring use of hypnotics show that, in 2010, around fifty million Americans were prescribed compounds like Ambien or Lunesta, and many millions more bought overthe-counter sleep products. But it would be misguided to imagine an amelioration of current conditions that would allow people to sleep soundly and wake refreshed. At this point in time, even a less oppressively organized world would not likely eliminate insomnia. Sleeplessness takes on its historical significance and its particular affective texture in relation to the collective experiences external to it, and insomnia is now inseparable from many other forms of dispossession and social ruin occurring globally. As an individual privation in our present, it is continuous with a generalized condition of worldlessness.

The philosopher Emmanuel Levinas is one of several thinkers who have tried to engage the meanings of insomnia in the context of recent history.[7] Insomnia, he argues, is a way of imagining the extreme difficulty of individual responsibility in the face of the catastrophes of our era. Part of the modernized world we inhabit is the ubiquitous visibility of useless violence and the human suffering it causes. This visibility, in all its mixed forms, is a glare that ought to thoroughly disturb any complacency, that ought to preclude the restful unmindfulness of sleep. Insomnia corresponds to the necessity of vigilance, to a refusal to overlook the horror and injustice that pervades the world. It is the disquiet of the effort to avoid inattention to the torment of the other. But its disquiet is also the frustrating inefficacy of an ethic of watchfulness; the act of witnessing and its monotony can become a mere enduring of the night, of the disaster. It is neither in public nor fully private. For Levinas, insomnia always hovers between a self-absorption and a radical depersonalization; it does not exclude a concern for the other, but it provides no clear sense of a space for the other's presence. It is where we face the near impossibility of living humanely. For sleeplessness must be distinguished from an unrelieved wakefulness, with its almost unbearable attention to suffering and the boundlessness of responsibility that would impose.

A 24/7 world is a disenchanted one in its eradication of shadows and obscurity and of alternate temporalities. It is a world identical to itself, a world with the shallowest of pasts, and thus in principle without specters. But the homogeneity of the present is an effect of the fraudulent brightness that presumes to extend everywhere and to preempt any mystery or unknowability. A 24/7 world produces an apparent equivalence between what is immediately available, accessible, or utilizable and what exists. The spectral is, in some way, the intrusion or disruption of the present by something out of time and by the ghosts of what has not been deleted by modernity, of victims who will not be forgotten, of unfulfilled emancipation. The routines of 24/7 can neutralize or absorb many dislocating experiences of return that could potentially undermine the substantiality and identity of the present and its apparent self-sufficiency. One of the most prescient engagements with the place of the spectral in an illuminated world without day or night is Andrei Tarkovsky's 1972 film *Solaris*. It is the story of several scientists on a spacecraft orbiting an enigmatic alien planet to observe its activity for possible inconsistencies with existing scientific theory. For the inhabitants of the brightly lit and artificial environment of the space station, insomnia is a chronic condition. In this milieu, inimical to rest or retreat, and in which one lives exposed and externalized, there is a breakdown of cognitive control. Under the extremity of these conditions, one is overtaken not just by hallucinations but by the presence of ghosts, in the film referred to as "visitors." The sensory impoverishment of the space station environment and the loss of diurnal time loosen one's psychic hold on a stable present, allowing dream as the bearer of memory to be relocated into waking life. For Tarkovsky, this proximity of the spectral and the living force of remembrance enables one to remain human in an inhuman world, and makes sleeplessness and exposure bearable. Coming as it did in the tentative spaces of cultural experiment in the early 1970s Soviet Union, *Solaris* shows that to acknowledge and affirm these ghostly returns, after repeated denials and repressions, is a pathway toward the attainability of freedom or happiness.

A current in contemporary political theory posits exposure as a fundamental or transhistorical feature of what has always constituted an individual. Rather than being autonomous or self-sufficient, an individual cannot be understood except in relation to what is outside them, to an otherness that faces them.[8] Only around this state of vulnerability can there be an opening onto the dependencies by which society is sustained. However, we are now at a historical moment when this bare condition of exposure has been unhinged from its relation to communal forms that at least tentatively offered safekeeping or care. Especially relevant here is the exploration of these problems in the work of Hannah Arendt. Over many years, she used figures of light and visibility in her accounts of what was necessary for there to be any substantive political life. For an individual to have political effectiveness, there needed to be a balance, a moving back and forth between the bright, even harsh exposure of public activity and the protected, shielded sphere of domestic or private life, of what she calls "the darkness of sheltered existence." Elsewhere she refers to "the twilight that suffuses our private and intimate lives." Without that space or time of privacy, away from "the implacable bright light of the constant presence of others on the public scene," there could be no possibility of the nurturing of the singularity of the self, a self that could make a substantive contribution to exchanges about the common good.

For Arendt, the private sphere had to be distinct from the individual pursuit of material happiness in which the self is defined through acquisitiveness, and by what it consumes. In

The Human Condition she elaborated these two realms in terms of a rhythmic balance between exhaustion and regeneration: the exhaustion resulting from labor or activity in the world, and the regeneration that regularly occurs within an enclosed and shaded domesticity. Arendt was well aware that her model of mutually sustaining relations between public and private had only infrequently been historically actualized. But she saw even the possibilities of such a balance profoundly threatened by the rise of an economy in which "things must be almost as quickly devoured and discarded as they have appeared in the world," making impossible any shared recognition of common interests or goals. Writing in the midst of the Cold War 1950s, she had the perspicacity to say: if "we were truly nothing but members of a consumer society we would no longer live in a world at all, we would simply be driven by a process in whose ever-recurring cycles things appear and disappear."[9] She was equally cognizant of how public life and the sphere of work were for most people experiences of estrangement.

There are many familiar and related utterances, from William Blake's "May God us keep from single vision and Newton's sleep," Carlyle's "over our noblest faculties is spreading a nightmare sleep," and Emerson's "sleep lingers all our lifetime about our eyes," to Guy Debord's "The spectacle expresses nothing more than society's wish for sleep." It would be easy to accumulate hundreds of other examples of this inverted characterization of the *waking* portion of modern social experience. Images of a society of sleepers come from

22

the left and right, from high culture and low, and have been a constant feature of cinema from *Caligari* to *The Matrix*. Common to these evocations of mass somnambulance is the suggestion of impaired or diminished *perceptual* capabilities combined with routinized, habitual, or trance-like behavior. Most mainstream social theory prescribes that modern individuals live and act, at least intermittently, in states that are emphatically unsleeplike—states of self-awareness in which one has the ability to evaluate events and information as a rational and objective participant in public or civic life. Any positions that characterize people as bereft of agency, as passive automatons open to manipulation or behavioral management, are usually deemed reductive or irresponsible.

At the same time, most notions of political awakenings are considered equally disturbing, in that they imply a sudden and irrational conversion-like process. One has only to remember the main election slogan of the Nazi Party in the early 1930s: "Deutschland Erwache!" Germany awake! More remote historically is Saint Paul's Letter to the Romans: "Knowing the time, that now it is high time to awake out of sleep . . . let us cast off the works of darkness and put on the armor of light." Or more recently and tediously, the call by anti-Ceauçescu forces in 1989: "Awake Romanians from the deep sleep put upon you by a tyrant's hands." Political and religious awakenings are usually articulated in perceptual terms as a newfound ability to see through a veil to a true state of things, to discriminate an inverted world from one right-side-up, or to recover a lost truth that becomes the negation of whatever one has awoken from.

An epiphanic disturbance of the numbed blandness of routine existence, to wake is to recover authenticity as opposed to the numbed vacancy of sleep. In this sense, awakening is a form of decisionism: the experience of a redemptive moment that seems to disrupt historical time, in which an individual undergoes a self-transforming encounter with a previously unknown future. But this whole category of figures and metaphors is now incongruous in the face of a global system that never sleeps, as if to ensure that no potentially disturbing awakening is ever necessary or relevant. If anything survives of the iconography of dawn and sunrise, it is around what Nietzsche identified as the demand, formulated by Socrates, for a "permanent daylight of reason."[10] But since Nietzsche's time, there has been an enormous and irreversible transfer of human "reason" to the 24/7 operations of information processing networks, and to the unending transmission of light through fiber-optic circuitry.

Paradoxically, sleep is a figure for a subjectivity on which power can operate with the least political resistance *and* a condition that finally cannot be instrumentalized or controlled externally—that evades or frustrates the demands of global consumer society. Thus it hardly needs to be said that the many clichés in social and cultural discourse depend on a monolithic or fatuous sense of sleep. Maurice Blanchot, Maurice Merleau-Ponty, and Walter Benjamin are only a few of the twentieth-century thinkers who have meditated on the profound ambiguity of sleep and on the impossibility of positioning it in any binary schema. Clearly, sleep needs to be understood in relation to distinctions between private and public, between the individual and the collective, but always in recognition of their permeability and proximity. The larger thrust of my argument is that, in the context of our own present, sleep can stand for the durability of the social, and that sleep might be analogous to other thresholds at which society could defend or protect itself. As the most private, most vulnerable state common to all, sleep is crucially dependent on society in order to be sustained.

In Thomas Hobbes's *Leviathan*, one of the vivid examples of the insecurity of the state of nature is the defenselessness of an individual sleeper against the numerous perils and predators to be feared on a nightly basis. Thus, a rudimentary obligation of the commonwealth is to provide security for the sleeper, not only from actual dangers but—equally important—from anxiety about them. The protection for the sleeper provided by the commonwealth occurs within a larger refiguring of the social relation between security and sleep. At the outset of the seventeenth century, one finds the remains of an imagined hierarchy that distinguished the more-than-human capabilities of a lord or sovereign whose omniscient powers, at least symbolically, did not succumb to the disabling conditions of sleep, from the somatic instincts of ordinary toiling men and women. However, in Shakespeare's *Henry the Fifth* and Cervantes's *Don Quixote* one finds both the articulation and the hollowing out of this hierarchical model. For King Henry, the relevant distinction is not simply between sleep and wakefulness, but between a perceptual vigilance sustained throughout "the all-watched night" and the sound slumber and "vacant mind" of the yeomen or peasant. Sancho Panza, from a different vantage point, divides the world into those, like himself, who were born to sleep and those, like his master, who were born to watch. In both texts, even though the obligations associated with rank superficially survive, there is a parallel awareness of the obsolescence and merely formal persistence of this paternalistic model of watchfulness.

Hobbes's work is an important indication of a transformation in both the guarantee of security and the needs of the sleeper. New kinds of dangers have displaced those that concerned Henry and the master of Sancho Panza, and these perils are addressed in a contractual arrangement no longer founded on a natural order of earthly and heavenly positions. The great inaugural bourgeois republics, like Hobbes's imagined commonwealth, were exclusionary in that they existed to serve the needs of propertied classes. Thus the security offered to the sleeper turns not simply on physical or bodily safety, but on the protection of property and goods while one slept. Also, the potential menace to the peaceful sleep of the ownership class comes from the poor and indigent, whereas the lowliest, even the "wretched slave," were fully included among the sleepers over whom King Henry was obliged to keep watch. The relationship between property and the right or privilege of restful sleep has its origins in the seventeenth century, and remains in force today in the cities of the twenty-first century. Public spaces are now comprehensively planned to deter sleeping, often including—with an intrinsic cruelty—the serrated design of benches and other elevated surfaces that prevent a human body from reclining on them. The pervasive but socially disregarded phenomenon of urban homelessness entails many deprivations, yet few are more acute than the hazards and insecurities of unsheltered sleep.

In a larger sense, however, the contract that purported to offer protection for anyone, whether propertied or not, has long been broken. In Kafka's work we find the ubiquity of the conditions that Arendt identified as the absence of spaces or times in which there can be repose and regeneration. *The Castle*, "The Burrow," and other texts repeatedly convey a sense of the insomnia and the obligatory watchfulness that accompany modern forms of isolation and estrangement. In *The Castle* there is a reversal of the older model of sovereign protection: here the desultory vigilance and enervating wakefulness of the Land Surveyor mark his inferiority and irrelevance to the slumbering officials of the castle bureaucracy. Kafka's "The Burrow," a tale of creaturely existence reduced to the obsessive and anxious pursuit of self-preservation, is one of the bleakest portrayals in literature of life as a solitude cut off from any mutuality. It is a dark prospectus of human life in the absence of community or civil society, at a furthest remove from the collective forms of living in the recently established kibbutzim, to which Kafka was so attracted.

The devastating reality of the absence of protection or security for those most in need of it was horrifyingly evident in the 1984 Bhopal chemical plant disaster in India. Shortly after midnight on December 1, a leak of highly toxic gas from a

27

poorly maintained storage tank killed tens of thousands of nearby residents, most of them sleeping at the time. Many thousands more died over the weeks and months following, with an even greater number injured and disabled permanently. Bhopal remains a stark disclosure of the discordance between corporate globalization and the possibility of security and sustainability for human communities. In the decades since 1984, the continuing repudiation by Union Carbide of any responsibility or of justice for the victims confirms that the disaster itself cannot be posed as an accident, and that, in the context of corporate operations, the victims were inherently superfluous. Certainly, the consequences of the incident would have been equally horrific had it occurred in daytime, but that it did take place at night underscores the unique vulnerability of the sleeper in a world from which long-standing social safeguards have vanished, or where they have been debilitated. A number of fundamental assumptions about the cohesion of social relations come together around the issue of sleep—in the reciprocity between vulnerability and trust, between exposure and care. Crucial is the dependence on the safekeeping of others for the revivifying carelessness of sleep, for a periodic interval of being free of fears, and for a temporary "forgetfulness of evil."[11] As the corrosion of sleep intensifies, it may become clearer how the solicitude that is essential for the sleeper is not qualitatively different from the protectiveness that is required by more immediately obvious and acute forms of social suffering.

CHAPTER TWO

24/7 announces a time without time, a time extracted from any material or identifiable demarcations, a time without sequence or recurrence. In its peremptory reductiveness, it celebrates a hallucination of presence, of an unalterable permanence composed of incessant, frictionless operations. It belongs to the aftermath of a common life made into the object of technics. It also resonates indirectly but powerfully as an injunction, as what some theorists call an "order-word." Deleuze and Guattari describe the "mot d'ordre" as a command, as an instrumentalization of language that aims either to preserve or to create social reality, and whose effect, finally, is to create fear.[1] In spite of its insubstantiality and abstraction as a slogan, the implacability of 24/7 is its impossible temporality. It is always a reprimand and a deprecation of the weakness and inadequacy of human time, with its blurred, meandering textures. It effaces the relevance or value of any respite or variability. Its heralding of the convenience of perpetual access conceals its cancellation of the periodicity that shaped the life of most cultures for several millennia: the diurnal pulse of waking and sleeping and the longer alternations between days of work and a day of worship or rest, which for the ancient Mesopotamians, Hebrews, and others became a seven-day week. In other ancient cultures, in Rome and in Egypt, there were eight- and ten-day weeks organized around market days or the quarter phases of the moon. The weekend is the modern residue of those long-standing systems, but even this marking of temporal differentiation is eroded by the imposition of 24/7 homogeneity. Of course, these earlier distinctions (the individual days of the week, holidays, seasonal breaks) persist, but their significance and legibility is being effaced by the monotonous indistinction of 24/7.

If 24/7 can be provisionally conceptualized as an order-word, its force is not as a demand for actual compliance or conformity to its apodictic format. Rather, the effectiveness of 24/7 lies in the incompatibility it lays bare, in the discrepancy between a human life-world and the evocation of a switched-on universe for which no off-switch exists. Of course, no individual can ever be shopping, gaming, working, blogging, downloading, or texting 24/7. However, since no moment, place, or situation now exists in which one can *not* shop, consume, or exploit networked resources, there is a relentless incursion of the non-time of 24/7 into every aspect of social or personal life. There are, for example, almost no circumstances now that can *not* be recorded or archived as digital imagery or information. The promotion and adoption of wireless technologies, and their annihilation of the singularity of place and event, is simply an after-effect of new institutional requirements. In its despoliation of the rich textures and indeterminations of human time, 24/7 simultaneously incites an unsustainable and self-liquidating identification with its fantasmatic requirements; it solicits an open-ended but always unfinished investment in the many products for facilitating this identification. It does not eliminate experiences external to or unreliant on it, but it does impoverish and diminish them. The examples of how in-use devices and apparatuses have an impact on small-scale forms of sociality (a meal, a conversation, or a classroom) may have become commonplaces, but the cumulative harm sustained is nonetheless significant. One inhabits a world in which long-standing notions of shared experience atrophy, and yet one never actually attains the gratifications or rewards promised by the most recent technological options. In spite of the omnipresent proclamations of the compatibility, even harmonization, between human time and the temporalities of networked systems, the lived realities of this relationship are disjunctions, fractures, and continual disequilibrium.

Deleuze and Guattari went to the point of comparing the order-word to "a death sentence." Historically and rhetorically, it may have shed some of this original meaning, but a judgment thus enunciated continues to operate within a system in which power is exercised on bodies. They also note that the order-word is simultaneously "a warning cry [and] a message to flee." As an announcement of its absolute unliveability, 24/7 is comprehensible in terms of this two-sidedness. It not only incites in the individual subject an exclusive focus on getting, having, winning, gawking, squandering, and deriding, but is fully interwoven with mechanisms of control that maintain the superfluousness and powerlessness of the subject of its demands. The externalization of the individual into a site of non-stop scrutiny and regulation is effectively continuous with the organization of state terror and the military-police paradigm of full-spectrum dominance.

To take one of many examples, the expanded use of unmanned drone missiles has been made possible by an intelligence-gathering system which the US Air Force has named Operation Gorgon Stare. It refers to a collection of surveillance and data-analysis resources that "sees" unblinkingly 24/7, indifferent to day, night, or weather, and that is lethally oblivious to the specificity of the living beings it targets. The terror of 24/7 is evident not only in the drone attacks, but also in the ongoing practice of night raids by Special Forces, beginning in Iraq, and now in Afghanistan and elsewhere. Provided with logistical satellite intelligence from Gorgon Stare, outfitted with advanced night-vision equipment, and arriving without warning in low-noise stealth helicopters, US teams conduct night assaults on villages and settlements with the overt aim of targeted assassination. Both the drones and night raids have aroused extraordinary anger among the Afghan population, not only for their homicidal consequences but also for the calculated ruination of nighttime itself. Part of the larger strategic intent, in the context of tribal cultures in Afghanistan, is to shatter the communally shared interval of sleep and restoration, and impose in its place a permanent state of fearfulness from which escape is not possible. It is a parallel application of the psychological techniques deployed in Abu Ghraib and Guantánamo to a broader population that exploits the vulnerability of sleep and the social patterns sustaining it with mechanized forms of terror.

Even though I have made several characterizations of 24/7 around figures of a perpetual illumination, it is important to stress that these have a limited usefulness if taken literally; 24/7 denotes the wreckage of the day as much as it concerns the extinguishing of darkness and obscurity. Desolating any luminous conditions except those of functionality, 24/7 is part of an immense incapacitation of visual experience. It coincides with an omnipresent field of operations and expectations to which one is exposed and in which individual optical activity is made the object of observation and management. Within this field, the contingency and variability of the visible world are no longer accessible. The most important recent changes concern not new machine forms of visualization, but the ways in which there has been a disintegration of human abilities to see, especially of an ability to join visual discriminations with social and ethical valuations. With an infinite cafeteria of solicitation and attraction perpetually available, 24/7 disables vision through processes of homogenization, redundancy, and acceleration. Contrary to many claims, there is an ongoing diminution of mental and perceptual capabilities rather than their expansion or modulation. Current arrangements are comparable to the glare of high-intensity illumination or of white-out conditions, in which there is a paucity of tonal differentiation out of which one can make perceptual distinctions and orient oneself to shared temporalities. Glare here is not a phenomenon of literal brightness, but rather of the uninterrupted harshness of monotonous stimulation in which a larger range of responsive capacities are frozen or neutralized.

In Jean-Luc Godard's *In Praise of Love* (2001) an off-screen voice poses a question: "When did the gaze collapse?" ("Quand est-ce-que le regard a basculé?") and pursues a possible response with another question: "Was it ten years, fifteen years, or even fifty years ago, before television?" No specific answer is forthcoming, for in this and other recent films, Godard makes clear that the crisis of the observer and the image is a cumulative one, with overlapping historical roots, unrelated to any specific technologies. *In Praise of Love* is a meditation by Godard on memory, resistance, and intergenerational responsibility, and in it he makes clear that something fundamental has changed in the way in which we see, or fail to see, the world. Part of this failure, he suggests, stems from a damaged relation to the past and to memory. We are swamped with images and information about the past and its recent catastrophes—but there is also a growing incapacity to engage these traces in ways that could move beyond them, in the interest of a common future. Amid the mass amnesia sustained by the culture of global capitalism, images have become one of the many depleted and disposable elements that, in their intrinsic archiveability, end up never being discarded, contributing to an ever more congealed and future-less present. At times, Godard seems to hold out hope for the possibility of images that would be completely useless to capitalism, but, as much as anyone, he never overestimates the immunity of any image to recuperation and neutralization.

One of the most numbingly familiar assumptions in discussions of contemporary technological culture is that there has been an epochal shift in a relatively short period of time, in which new information and communication technologies have supplanted a broad set of older cultural forms. This historical break is described and theorized in various ways, involving accounts of a change from industrial production to post-industrial processes and services, from analog to digital media, or from a print-based culture to a global society unified by the instantaneous circulation of data and information. Most often, such periodizations depend on comparative parallels with earlier historical periods that are defined by specific technological innovations. Thus, accompanying the assertion that we have entered a new and unprecedented era, there is the reassuring insistence on a correspondence with, for example, "the Gutenberg era" or "the industrial revolution." In other words, accounts of rupture simultaneously affirm a continuity with larger patterns and sequences of technological change and innovation.

Often suggested is the notion that we are now in the midst of a transitional phase, passing from one "age" to another, and only at the beginnings of the latter. This presupposes an unsettled interlude of social and subjective adaptations lasting a generation or two, before a new era of relative stability is securely in place. One of the consequences of representing global contemporaneity in the form of a new technological epoch is the sense of historical inevitability attributed to changes in large-scale economic developments and in the micro-phenomena of everyday life. The idea of technological change as quasi-autonomous, driven by some process of auto-poesis or self-organization, allows many aspects of contemporary social reality to be accepted as necessary, unalterable circum-stances, akin to facts of nature. In the false placement of today's most visible products and devices within an explanatory line-age that includes the wheel, the pointed arch, movable type, and so forth, there is a concealment of the most important techniques invented in the last 150 years: the various systems for the management and control of human beings.

This pseudo-historical formulation of the present as a digital age, supposedly homologous with a "bronze age" or "steam age," perpetuates the illusion of a unifying and durable coher-ence to the many incommensurable constituents of contemporary experience. Of the numerous presentations of this delusion, the promotional and intellectually spurious works of futurists such as Nicholas Negroponte, Esther Dyson, Kevin Kelly, and Raymond Kurzweil can stand as flagrant examples. One of the underpinnings of this assumption is the popular truism that today's teenagers and younger children are all now harmoniously inhabiting the inclusive and seamless intelligibility of their technological worlds. This generational characterization supposedly confirms that, within another few decades or less, a transitional phase will have ended and there will be billions of individuals with a similar level of technological competence and basic intellectual assumptions. With a new paradigm fully in place, there will be innovation, but in this scenario it will occur within the stable and enduring conceptual and functional parameters of this "digital" epoch. However, the very different actuality of our time is the calculated maintenance of an ongoing state of transition. There never will be a "catching up" on either a social or individual basis in relation to continually changing technological requirements. For the vast majority of people, our perceptual and cognitive relationship to communication and information technology will continue to be estranged and disempowered because of the velocity at which new products emerge and at which arbitrary reconfigurations of entire systems take place. This intensified rhythm precludes the possibility of becoming familiar with any given arrangement. Certain cultural theorists insist that such conditions can easily be the basis for neutralizing institutional power, but actual evidence supporting this view is non-existent.

At a fundamental level, this is hardly a new state of affairs. The logic of economic modernization in play today can be traced directly back to the mid nineteenth century. Marx was one of the first to understand the intrinsic incompatibility of capitalism with stable or durable social forms, and the history of the last 150 years is inseparable from the "constant revolutionizing" of forms of production, circulation, communication, and image-making. However, during that century and a half, within specific areas of cultural and economic life, there were numerous intervals of apparent stability, when certain institutions and arrangements seemed abiding or long-lasting. For example, cinema, as a technological form, appeared to consist of some relatively fixed elements and relations from the late 1920s into the 1960s or even early 1970s. As I discuss in Chapter 3, television in the US seemed to have a material and experiential consistency from the 1950s into the 1970s. These periods, in which certain key features seemed to be permanent, allowed critics to expound theories of cinema, television, or video based on the assumption that these forms or systems had certain essential self-defining characteristics. In retrospect, what were most often identified as essential were temporary elements of larger constellations whose rates of change were variable and unpredictable.

In a related manner, many ambitious attempts have been made since the 1990s to articulate the defining or intrinsic manifestations of "new media." Even the most intelligent of these efforts are often limited by their implicit assumption, conditioned by studies of previous historical moments, that the key task is to outline and analyze a new technological/discursive paradigm or regime, and, most importantly, that this new regime is derivable from the actual devices, networks, apparatuses, codes, and global architectures now in place. But it must be emphasized that we are not, as such accounts suggest, simply passing from one dominant arrangement of machinic and discursive systems to another. That books and essays written on new media only five years ago are already outdated is particularly telling, and anything written with the same goal today will become dated in far less time. At present, the particular operation and effects of specific new machines or networks are less important than how the rhythms, speeds, and formats of accelerated and intensified consumption are reshaping experience and perception.

To take one of many possible examples from recent critical literature: several years ago a German media theorist proposed that the cell phone equipped with visual display represents a "revolutionary" break with previous technological forms, including all earlier telephones. He argued that, because of its mobility, the miniaturization of the screen, and its ability to display data and video, it was "a truly radical development." Even if one is inclined to approach technological history as sequences demarcated by inventions and breakthroughs, the relevance of this particular apparatus will be notably and inevitably short-lived. It is more useful to understand such a device as merely one element in a transient flux of compulsory and disposable products. Very different display formats are already on the near horizon, some involving the augmented realities of see-through interfaces and small head-worn devices, in which a virtual screen will be identical with one's field of vision. Also, there is the development of gesture-based computing in which, instead of a click, a wave, a nod, or the blink of an eye will suffice as a command. Before long these may well displace the apparent ubiquity and necessity of hand-held, touch-based devices, and thereby cancel any special historical claims for

what came before. But if and when such devices are introduced (and no doubt labeled as revolutionary), they will simply
be facilitating the perpetuation of the same banal exercise of
non-stop consumption, social isolation, and political powerlessness, rather than representing some historically significant
turning point. And they too will occupy only a brief interval of
currency before their inevitable replacement and transit to the
global waste piles of techno-trash. The only consistent factor
connecting the otherwise desultory succession of consumer
products and services is the intensifying integration of one's
time and activity into the parameters of electronic exchange.
Billions of dollars are spent every year researching how to
reduce decision-making time, how to eliminate the useless
time of reflection and contemplation. This is the form of
contemporary progress—the relentless capture and control of
time and experience.

As many have noted, the form that innovation takes within
capitalism is as the continual simulation of the new, while
existing relations of power and control remain effectively the
same. For much of the twentieth century, novelty production,
in spite of its repetitiveness and nullity, was often marketed to
coincide with a social imagination of a future more advanced
than, or at least unlike, the present. Within the framework of a
mid-twentieth-century futurism, the products one purchased
and fit into one's life seemed vaguely linked with popular
evocations of eventual global prosperity, automation benignly
displacing human labor, space exploration, the elimination of
crime and disease, and so on. There was at least the misplaced

belief in technological solutions to intractable social problems. Now the accelerated tempo of apparent change deletes any sense of an extended time frame that is shared collectively, which might sustain even a nebulous anticipation of a future distinct from contemporary reality. 24/7 is shaped around individual goals of competitiveness, advancement, acquisitiveness, personal security, and comfort at the expense of others. The future is so close at hand that it is imaginable only by its continuity with the striving for individual gain or survival in the shallowest of presents.

My argument may seem to contain two inconsistent threads. On one hand I am affirming, along with some other writers, that the shape of contemporary technological culture still corresponds to the logic of modernization as it unfolded in the later nineteenth century—that is to say, that some key features of early-twenty-first-century capitalism can still be linked with aspects of the industrial projects associated with Werner Siemens, Thomas Edison, and George Eastman. Their names can stand emblematically for the development of vertically integrated corporate empires that reshaped crucial aspects of social behavior. Their prescient ambitions were realized through (1) an understanding of human needs as always mutable and expandable, (2) an embryonic conception of the commodity as potentially convertible into abstract flows, whether of images, sounds, or energy, (3) effective measures to decrease circulation time, and (4) in the case of Eastman and Edison, an early but clear vision of the economic reciprocities between "hardware" and "software." The consequences of

41

these nineteenth-century models, especially the facilitation and maximization of content distribution, would impose themselves onto human life much more comprehensively throughout the twentieth century.

On the other hand, sometime in the late twentieth century it is possible to identify a constellation of forces and entities distinct from those of the nineteenth century and its sequential phases of modernization. By the 1990s, a thoroughgoing transformation of vertical integration had taken place, exemplified most familiarly by the innovations of Microsoft, Google, and others, even though some remnants of older hierarchical structures persisted alongside newer, more flexible and capillary models of implementation and control. Within this emerging context, technological consumption coincides with and becomes indistinguishable from strategies and effects of power. Certainly, for much of the twentieth century, the organization of consumer societies was never unconnected with forms of social regulation and subjection, but now the management of economic behavior is synonymous with the formation and perpetuation of malleable and assenting individuals. An older logic of planned obsolescence continues to operate, propelling the demand for replacement or enhancement. However, even if the dynamic behind product innovation is still linked to the rate of profit or to corporate competition for sector dominance, the heightened tempo of "improved" or reconfigured systems, models, and platforms is a crucial part of the remaking of a subject and of the intensification of control. Docility and separation are not indirect by-products of a financialized global economy, but are among its primary aims. There is an ever closer linking of individual needs with the functional and ideological programs in which each new product is embedded. "Products" are hardly just devices or physical apparatuses, but various services and interconnections that quickly become the dominant or exclusive ontological templates of one's social reality.

But this contemporary phenomenon of acceleration is not simply a linear succession of innovations in which there is a substitution of a new item for something out of date. Each replacement is always accompanied by an exponential increase beyond the previous number of choices and options. It is a continuous process of distension and expansion, occurring simultaneously on different levels and in different locations, a process in which there is a multiplication of the areas of time and experience that are annexed to new machinic tasks and demands. A logic of displacement (or obsolescence) is conjoined with a broadening and diversifying of the processes and flows to which an individual becomes effectively linked. Any apparent technological novelty is also a qualitative dilation of one's accommodation to and dependence on 24/7 routines; it is also part of an expansion in the number of points at which an individual is made into an *application* of new control systems and enterprises.

However, it must be said that, at present, individuals experience the workings of a global economy in very different ways. Within cosmopolitan sectors of the planet, the strategies of disempowerment using mandatory techniques of digital personalization and self-administration flourish even among very low-income groups. At the same time, there are vast numbers of human beings, barely at or below subsistence level, who cannot be integrated into the new requirements of markets, and they are irrelevant and expendable. Death, in many guises, is one of the by-products of neoliberalism: when people have nothing further that can be taken from them, whether resources or labor power, they are quite simply disposable. However, the current increase in sexual slavery and the growing traffic in organs and body parts suggest that the outer limit of disposability can be profitably enlarged to meet the demands of new market sectors.

This unrelenting rhythm of technological consumption, as it has developed over the past two or three decades, prevents any significant period of time elapsing in which the use of a given product, or assemblage of them, could become familiar enough to constitute merely the background elements of one's life. Operational and performative capabilities assume a priority that overrides the significance of anything that might once have been thought of as "content." Rather than being a means to a larger set of ends, the apparatus is the end itself. Its purpose is directing its user to an ever more efficient fulfillment of its own routine tasks and functions. It is systemically impossible that there might be a clearing or pause in which a longer-term time frame of trans-individual concerns and projects might come into view. The very brief lifespan of a given apparatus or arrangement encompasses the pleasure and prestige associated with its ownership, but simultaneously includes an awareness that the object at hand is tainted with impermanence and decay from the outset. Older cycles of replacement were at least long enough for the consensual illusion of semi-permanence to hold sway for a while. Now the brevity of the interlude before a high-tech product literally becomes garbage requires two contradictory attitudes to coexist: on one hand, the initial need and/or desire for the product, but, on the other, an affirmative identification with the process of inexorable cancellation and replacement. The acceleration of novelty production is a disabling of collective memory, and it means that the evaporation of historical knowledge no longer has to be implemented from the top down. The conditions of communication and information access on an everyday level ensure the systematic erasure of the past as part of the fantasmatic construction of the present.

Inevitably, such short cycles will, for some, produce anxieties about outmodedness and frustrations of various kinds. However it is important to acknowledge the attractive incitements to align oneself with a continually evolving sequence based on promises of enhanced functionality, even if any substantive benefits are always deferred. At present, the desire to accumulate objects is less important than the confirmation that one's life is coinciding with whatever applications, devices, or networks are, at any given moment, available and heavily promoted. From this vantage point, accelerated patterns of acquiring and discarding are never something regrettable, but rather a tangible sign of one's access to the flows and capabilities most in demand. Following Boltanski and Chiapello, social phenomena that are characterized by the appearance of

45

stasis or slow rates of change are marginalized and drained of value or desirability. Committing to activities where time spent cannot be leveraged through an interface and its links is now something to be avoided or done sparingly.

Submission to these arrangements is near irresistible because of the portent of social and economic failure—the fear of falling behind, of being deemed outdated. The rhythms of technological consumption are inseparable from the requirement of continual self-administration. Every new product or service presents itself as essential for the bureaucratic organization of one's life, and there is an ever-growing number of routines and needs that constitute this life that no one has actually chosen. The privatization and compartmentalization of one's activities in this sphere are able to sustain the illusion one can "outwit the system" and devise a unique or superior relation to these tasks that is either more enterprising or seemingly less compromised. The myth of the lone hacker perpetuates the fantasy that the asymmetrical relation of individual to network can be creatively played to the former's advantage. In actuality there is an imposed and inescapable uniformity to our compulsory labor of self-management. The illusion of choice and autonomy is one of the foundations of this global system of auto-regulation. In many places one still encounters the assertion that contemporary technological arrangements are essentially a neutral set of tools that can be used in many different ways, including in the service of an emancipatory politics. The philosopher Giorgio Agamben has refuted such claims, countering that "today there is not even a single instant in which the life of individuals is not modeled, contaminated or controlled by some apparatus." He contends convincingly that "it is impossible for the subject of an apparatus to use it 'in the right way.' Those who continue to promote similar arguments are, for their part, the product of the media apparatus in which they are captured."[2]

To be preoccupied with the aesthetic properties of digital imagery, as are many theorists and critics, is to evade the subordination of the image to a broad field of non-visual operations and requirements. Most images are now produced and circulated in the service of maximizing the amount of time spent in habitual forms of individual self-management and self-regulation. Fredric Jameson has argued that, with the breakdown of significant distinctions between what had been the spheres of work and leisure, the imperative to look at images is central to the functioning of most hegemonic institutions today. He indicates how mass culture imagery up to the mid twentieth century often provided ways of evading the prohibitions of a super-ego.[3] Now in a reversal, the demand for mandatory 24/7 immersion in visual content effectively becomes a new form of institutional super-ego. Of course, more images, of many kinds, are looked at, are seen, than ever before, but it is within what Foucault has described as a "network of permanent observation." Most of the historically accumulated understandings of the term "observer" are destabilized under such conditions: that is, when individual acts of vision are unendingly solicited for conversion into information that will both enhance technologies of control *and* be a form of surplus value in a marketplace based on the accumulation of data on user behavior. There is a much more literal overturning of assumptions about the position and agency of an observer in the expanding array of technical means for making acts of seeing themselves into objects of observation.

The most advanced forms of surveillance and data analysis used by intelligence agencies are now equally indispensable to the marketing strategies of large businesses. Widely employed are screens or other forms of display that track eye movements, as well as durations and fixations of visual interest in sequences or streams of graphic information. One's casual perusal of a single web page can be minutely analyzed and quantified in terms of how the eye scans, pauses, moves, and gives attentive priority to some areas over others. Even in the ambulatory space of big department stores, eye-tracking scanners provide detailed information about individual behavior—for example, determining how long one looked at items that one did *not* buy. A generously funded research field of optical ergonomics has been in place for some time. Passively and often voluntarily, one now collaborates in one's own surveillance and data-mining. This inevitably spirals into more fine-grained procedures for intervention in both individual and collective behavior. At the same time, images are essentially continuous with all the non-visual forms of information that one engages regularly. An instrumentalized sensory perception is merely one accompanying element in the accumulated activities of accessing, storage, formatting, manipulation, circulation, and exchange. Incalculable streams of images are omnipresent

24/7, but what finally occupies individual attention is the management of the technical conditions that surround them: all the expanding determinations of delivery, display, format, storage, upgrades, and accessories.

Everywhere one encounters the complacent and preposterous assumption that these systemic patterns are "here to stay," and that such levels of technological consumption are extendable to a planetary population of seven going on ten billion. Many who celebrate the transformative potential of communication networks are oblivious to the oppressive forms of human labor and environmental ravages on which their fantasies of virtuality and dematerialization depend. Even among the plural voices affirming that "another world is possible," there is often the expedient misconception that economic justice, mitigation of climate change, and egalitarian social relations can somehow occur alongside the continued existence of corporations like Google, Apple, and General Electric. Challenges to these delusions encounter intellectual policing of many kinds. There is an effective prohibition not only on the critique of mandatory technological consumption but also on the articulation of how existing technical capabilities and premises could be deployed in the service of human and social needs, rather than the requirements of capital and empire. The narrow and monopolized set of electronic products and services available at any given moment masquerades as the all-enveloping phenomenon of "technology." Even a partial refusal of the intensively marketed offerings of multinational corporations is construed as opposition to technology itself. To characterize current arrangements, in reality untenable and unsustainable, as anything but inevitable and unalterable is a contemporary heresy. It is impermissible for there to be credible or visible options of living outside the demands of 24/7 communication and consumption. Any questioning or discrediting of what is currently the most efficient means of producing acquiescence and docility, of promoting self-interest as the raison d'être of all social activity, is rigorously marginalized. To articulate strategies of living that would delink technology from a logic of greed, accumulation, and environmental despoliation merits sustained forms of institutional prohibition. Notably, the task of such policing is undertaken by that class of academics and critics that Paul Nizan called *les chiens de garde*: today the watchdogs are those technophilic intellectuals and writers anxious to qualify for media attention and eager for rewards and access from those in power. Of course, there are many other powerful obstacles to the public imagination of creative relations between technology and social reality.

Philosopher Bernard Stiegler has written widely on the consequences of what he sees as the homogenization of perceptual experience within contemporary culture.[4] He is especially concerned with the global circulation of mass-produced "temporal objects," which, for him, include movies, television programs, popular music, and video clips. Stiegler cites the advent of widespread internet use in the mid 1990s as a decisive turning point (his key date is 1992) in the impact of these industrial audiovisual products. Over the last two decades, he believes, they have been responsible for a "mass synchroniza-tion" of consciousness and memory. The standardization of experience on such a large scale, he argues, entails a loss of subjective identity and singularity; it also leads to the disastrous disappearance of individual participation and creativity in the making of the symbols we all exchange and share. His notion of synchronization is radically unlike what I referred to earlier as shared temporalities, in which the co-presence of differ-ences and otherness could be the basis for provisional publics or communities. Stiegler concludes there is an ongoing destruction of the "primordial narcissism" essential for a human being to care for themselves or for others, and he points to the many episodes of mass murder/suicide as ominous results of this widespread psychic and existential damage.[5] He calls urgently for the creation of counter-products that might reintroduce singularity into cultural experience and somehow disconnect desire from the imperatives of consumption.

Stiegler's work is representative of a broader shift away from more celebratory accounts in the mid 1990s of the relation between globalization and new information technologies. There were many then who predicted the opening up of a multicultural world of local rationalities, of a diasporic and multi-centered pluralism, based on electronic public spheres. In Stiegler's view, hopes for such developments were based on a misunderstanding of what was driving many processes of globalization. For him, the 1990s opened onto a hyper-indus-trial era, not a post-industrial one, in which a logic of mass production was suddenly aligned with techniques that, in unprecedented ways, combine fabrication, distribution, and subjectivation on a planetary scale.

While much of Stiegler's argument is compelling, I believe that the problem of "temporal objects" is secondary to the larger systemic colonization of individual experience that I have been discussing. Most important now is not the capture of attentiveness by a delimited object—a movie, television program, or piece of music—whose mass reception seems to be Stiegler's main preoccupation, but rather the remaking of attention into repetitive operations and responses that always overlap with acts of looking or listening. It is less the homogeneity of media products that perpetuates the separation, isolation, and neutralization of individuals than the larger and compulsory arrangements within which these elements, and many others, are consumed. Visual and auditory "content" is most often ephemeral, interchangeable material that, in addition to its commodity status, circulates to habituate and validate one's immersion in the exigencies of twenty-first-century capitalism. Stiegler tends to characterize audiovisual media in terms of a relatively passive model of reception, drawn in some respects from the phenomenon of broadcast television. One of his telling examples is the final match of the soccer World Cup, when billions literally watch the same images on TV simultaneously. But this notion of reception disregards the status of current media products as resources to be actively managed and manipulated, exchanged, reviewed, archived, recommended, "followed." Any act of viewing is layered with options of simultaneous and interruptive actions, choices, and feedback. The idea of long blocks of time spent exclusively as a spectator is outmoded. This time is far too valuable not to be leveraged with plural sources of solicitation and choices that maximize possibilities of monetization and that allow the continuous accumulation of information about the user.

It is also important to consider other omnipresent electronic industries of temporal objects, though ones that are more open-ended and indeterminate in their effects: for example, online gambling, internet pornography, and video-gaming. The drives and appetites at stake here, with their illusions of mastery, winning and possession, are crucial models for the intensification of 24/7 consumption. An extended examination of these more volatile forms would likely complicate Stiegler's conclusions about the capture of desire or the collapse of primordial narcissism. Admittedly, Stiegler's postulation of a global mass synchronization is nuanced, hardly reducible to the notion of everyone thinking or doing the same thing; and it is based on a sustained, if recondite, phenomenology of retention and memory. Nonetheless, against his idea of the industrial homogenization of consciousness and its flows, one can counterpose the parcellization and fragmentation of shared zones of experience into fabricated microworlds of affects and symbols. The unfathomable amount of accessible information can be deployed and arranged in the service of anything, personal or political, however aberrant or conventional. Through the unlimited possibilities of filtering and customization, individuals in close physical proximity can inhabit incommensurable and non-communicating universes. However, the vast majority of these microworlds, despite their patently different content, have a monotonous sameness in their temporal patterns and segmentations.

There are other contemporary forms of mass synchronization not directly tied to communication and information networks. A crucial example would be many of the consequences of the global traffic in pyschoactive drugs, both legal and illegal, including the growing blurred area between them (painkillers, tranquilizers, amphetamines, and so on). The hundreds of millions of people taking new compounds for depression, bipolar conditions, hyperactivity, and numerous other designations make up various aggregates of individuals whose nervous systems have been similarly modified. The same can obviously be said of the enormous constituencies, on every continent, buying and using illegal substances, whether opiates and coca derivatives or the proliferating number of designer drugs. Thus, on one hand, there is a vague uniformity of response and behavior among the users of a specific pharmaceutical product; but, on the other, there is the global patchwork of different drug-using populations, often physically proximate, but made up of highly disparate affects, drives, and incapacitations. The same difficulty arises with the problem of drugs as with that of media objects—the impossibility and the irrelevance of isolating any single determinant as responsible for the alteration of consciousness. There are shifting and indistinct composites of elements in the ingestion of both electronic flows and neuro-chemicals.

54

My intention is not to address the huge topic of the relation between drugs and media—or to test the familiar hypothesis that every medium is a drug, and vice versa. Rather, I want to stress how the patterns of consumption generated by current media and communication products are also present in other expanding global marketplaces—for example, in the ones controlled by major pharmaceutical corporations. Here too is a related acceleration of the tempo at which new and supposedly upgraded products are introduced. At the same time, there is a multiplication of the physical or psychological states for which new drugs are developed and then promoted as effective and obligatory treatments. As with digital devices and services, there is a fabrication of pseudo-necessities, or deficiencies for which new commodities are essential solutions. In addition, the pharmaceutical industry, in partnership with the neurosciences, is a vivid example of the financialization and externalization of what used to be thought of as "inner life." Over the last two decades, a growing range of emotional states have been incrementally pathologized in order to create vast new markets for previously unneeded products. The fluctuating textures of human affect and emotion that are only imprecisely suggested by the notions of shyness, anxiety, variable sexual desire, distraction, or sadness have been falsely converted into medical disorders to be targeted by hugely profitable drugs.

Of the many links between the use of psychotropic drugs and communication devices, one is their parallel production of forms of social compliance. But emphasizing only docility and tranquillization bypasses the fantasies of agency and enterprise also underpinning the markets for both these categories of products. For example, the widespread adult use of ADHD drugs is often driven by the hope of enhancing one's performance and competitiveness in the workplace—and, more harshly, methamphetamine addiction is often linked to destructive delusions about performance and self-aggrandizement. A generalized sameness is inevitably one result of the global scale of the markets in question, and their dependence on the consistent or predictable actions of large populations. It is attained *not* by the making of similar individuals, as theories of mass society used to assert, but through the reduction or elimination of differences, by narrowing the range of behaviors that can function effectively or successfully in most contemporary institutional contexts. Thus, above a relatively low economic stratum, a new blandness flourishes almost everywhere that accelerated consumption has become normalized—not just in certain professional strata, social groups, or age groups. Paul Valéry foresaw some of this as early as the 1920s in his understanding that technocratic civilization would eventually eliminate any ill-defined or incommensurable form of life within its spheres of operation.[6] To be bland is a becoming "smooth," as distinct from the idea of a mold that the word "conformity" often implies. Deviations are flattened or effaced, leading to that which is "neither irritating nor invigorating." (OED) This has been most evident over the last decade or so in the disappearance or domestication of what once constituted a much wider range of the markers of cultural marginality or outsider status. The omnipresence of 24/7 milieus is one of the conditions for this flattening, but 24/7 should be understood not simply as a homogenous and unvariegated time, but rather as a disabled and derelict diachrony. Certainly, there are differentiated temporalities, but the range and depth of distinctions between them diminishes, and an unimpeded substitutability between times becomes normalized. Conventional and older durational units persist (like "nine to five" or "Monday to Friday"), but overlaid onto them are all the practices of individual time management made possible by 24/7 networks and markets.

In the past, forms of repetitive labor, in spite of their tedium or oppressiveness, have not always precluded satisfactions derived from one's limited mastery or efficient operation of tools or machinery. As some historians have shown, modern systems of labor could not have flourished without the cultivation of new values in the context of industrialization to replace the ones that had sustained craft or artisanal work. The possibility of a sense of accomplishment in some end product of one's work became less and less tenable in large factory conditions. Instead, there arose ways of encouraging an identification with machinic processes themselves. Part of the culture of modernity took shape around various affirmations that there could be individual gratification from emulating the impervious rhythms, efficiency, and dynamism of mechanization. However, what were often ambivalent or merely symbolic compensations in the nineteenth and twentieth centuries have become a more intensive set of both real and imagined satisfactions. Because of the permeability, even indistinction, between the times of work and of leisure, the skills and gestures that once would have been restricted to the workplace are now a universal part of the 24/7 texture of one's electronic life. The ubiquity of technological interfaces inevitably leads users to strive for increasing fluency and adeptness. But the proficiency one acquires with each particular application or tool is effectively a greater harmonization with the intrinsic functional requirement continually to reduce the time of any exchange or operation. Apparatuses solicit a seemingly frictionless handling, dexterity, and know-how that is self-satisfying, and that can also impress others as a superior ability to make efficient or rewarding use of technological resources. The sense of individual ingenuity provides the temporary conviction that one is on the winning side of the system, somehow coming out ahead; but in the end there is a generalized leveling of all users into interchangeable objects of the same mass dispossession of time and praxis.

Individual habituation to these tempos has had devastating social and environmental consequences, and has produced a collective normalization of this ceaseless displacement and discarding. Because loss is continually created, an atrophied memory ceases to recognize it as such. The primary self-narration of one's life shifts in its fundamental composition. Instead of a formulaic sequence of places and events associated with family, work, and relationships, the main thread of one's life-story now is the electronic commodities and media services through which all experience has been filtered, recorded, or constructed. As the possibility of a single lifetime job vanishes, the enduring lifework available for most is the elaboration of one's relation to apparatuses. Everything once loosely considered to be "personal" is now reconfigured so as to facilitate the fabricating of oneself into a jumble of identities that exist only as effects of temporary technological arrangements.

The frameworks through which the world can be understood continue to be depleted of complexity, drained of whatever is unplanned or unforeseen. So many long-standing and multivalent forms of social exchange have been remade into habitual sequences of solicitation and response. At the same time, the range of what constitutes response becomes formulaic and, in most instances, is reduced to a small inventory of possible gestures or choices. Because one's bank account and one's friendships can now be managed through identical machinic operations and gestures, there is a growing homogenization of what used to be entirely unrelated areas of experience. At the same time, whatever remaining pockets of everyday life are not directed toward quantitative or acquisitive ends, or cannot be adapted to telematic participation, tend to deteriorate in esteem and desirability. Real-life activities that do not have an online correlate begin to atrophy, or cease to be relevant. There is an insurmountable asymmetry that degrades any local event or exchange. Because of the infinity of content accessible 24/7, there will always be something online more informative, surprising, funny, diverting, impressive than anything in one's immediate actual circumstances. It is now a given that a limitless availability of information or images can trump or override any human-scale communication or exploration of ideas.

According to the Tiqqun collective, we have become the innocuous, pliable inhabitants of global urban societies.[7] Even in the absence of any direct compulsion, we choose to do what we are told to do; we allow the management of our bodies, our ideas, our entertainment, and all our imaginary needs to be externally imposed. We buy products that have been recommended to us through the monitoring of our electronic lives, and then we voluntarily leave feedback for others about what we have purchased. We are the compliant subject who submits to all manner of biometric and surveillance intrusion, and who ingests toxic food and water and lives near nuclear reactors without complaint. The absolute abdication of responsibility for living is indicated by the titles of the many bestselling guides that tell us, with a grim fatality, the 1,000 movies to see before we die, the 100 tourist destinations to visit before we die, the 500 books to read before we die.

CHAPTER THREE

In a well-known work of art there are some significant and early anticipations of the 24/7 temporalities discussed so far. The British artist Joseph Wright of Derby produced a painting around 1782 titled *Arkwright's Cotton Mills by Night*. It has been reproduced in many books on the history of industrialization, to illustrate—often misleadingly—the impact of factory production on rural England (an impact that was not widely felt for many decades). The painting's strangeness comes in part from the understated but distinctly anti-picturesque implantation of six- and seven-story brick buildings within an otherwise untamed and wooded countryside. As historians have noted, they are structures without precedent in English architecture. Most unsettling, however, is the elaboration of a nocturnal scene in which the light of a full moon illuminating a cloud-filled sky coexists with the pin-points of windows lit by gas lamps in the cotton mills. The artificial lighting of the factories announces the rationalized deployment of an abstract relation between time and work, severed from the cyclical temporalities of lunar and solar movements. The novelty of Arkwright's mills is not a mechanical determinant, like the steam engine (they were powered exclusively by water) or the recently fabricated spinning frames. Instead, it is a radical reconceptualization of the relation between work and time: it is the idea of productive operations that do not stop, of profit-generating work that can function 24/7. At the particular site shown in the painting, a human labor force, including many children, was set to work at the machines in continuous twelve-hour shifts. Marx understood how capitalism was inseparable from this reorganization of time, specifically the time of living labor, as a way of creating surplus value, and he cited the words of Andrew Ure, the Scottish advocate of industrial rationalization, to amplify its importance: it was "the training of human beings to renounce their desultory habits of work, and to identify themselves with the unvarying regularity of the complex automaton. To devise and administer a successful code of factory diligence was the Herculean enterprise and noble achievement of Arkwright."[1]

The spectral disjunctions in Wright of Derby's image underscore Marx's account of capitalism's dissonant relation to the agrarian milieus in which it arose. Agriculture, Marx insisted, "could never be the sphere in which capitalism starts, the sphere in which it takes up its original residence."[2] The cyclical temporalities, whether seasonal or diurnal, around which farming had always been based constituted an insurmountable set of resistances to the remaking of labor time on which capitalism depended fundamentally from the start. The "natural conditions" of agrarian life prevented the necessary control over the time of production; hence the need for an unprecedented "residence," unencumbered by the long weight of customs and rhythms that reached far back into prehistory. The first requirement of capitalism, he wrote, was the dissolution of the relation to the earth. The modern factory thus emerged as an autonomous space in which the organization of labor could be disconnected from family, community, environment, or any traditional interdependencies or associations. Agriculture, as Marx presciently observed, would only be able to be industrialized retroactively.

Arkwright's Cotton Mills conveys the physical proximity of these two spheres, one natural, one invented, and also a sense of their incommensurability and fatal incompatibility. Only after capitalism had established its abstract order everywhere else—in fact, only after the destruction of World War II— could it fully impose itself on agriculture, with a factory-farming model applied to both animals and crops. More recently, corporations such as Monsanto and Dupont have achieved the final overcoming of Marx's "natural conditions" with genetically modified and patented agricultural materials. But this relatively early image of an irreconcilable adjacency nonetheless counters the notion of an "industrial revolution" that devastated the countryside and quickly herded rural laborers into cities and factories. Instead there was a protracted and piecemeal deterioration of older forms and spaces.

To be clear, I am using Arkwright's mills, as visualized by Wright of Derby, to designate, not the rationalization of manufacturing, but a broader homogenization of time and a conceptualization of uninterrupted processes that override natural and social constraints. Clearly, over the next one hundred years, into the later nineteenth century, the actuality of factories operating twenty-four hours a day was the exception, not the rule. It was in other spheres of economic modernization that non-stop and denaturalized organizations of time became pervasive. Alongside the large-scale restructuring of labor and production in the 1800s were the intertwined projects essential to the growth of capital: the acceleration and control of both circulation time and communication time. During the late 1830s and 1840s these included the build-out of transportation routes, most importantly railroads, but also of canals, and of tunnels through mountain ranges, as well as the enhancement of steamship speed and performance. There was also the parallel development of telegraph networks, and this initial period saw the first wire transfers of money, in the mid 1840s, and the completion in 1850 of an underwater cable across the English Channel. Around 1858 Marx is able to make some of his crucial formulations on the significance of these developments: "Capital by its nature drives beyond every spatial barrier. Thus the creation of the physical conditions of exchange — of the means of communication and transport — the annihilation of space by time — becomes an extraordinary necessity for it."[3] Yet it must be emphasized that what was important for Marx's analysis was not simply the technological achievement of faster speeds for the shipment of goods or the attainment of near-instantaneous communications. Rather, if circulation was an essential process of capital, it was because of "the *constant continuity* of the process." In effect, Marx is positing 24/7 temporalities as fundamental to the workings of capital; he understood that these durational processes were also metamorphic. Within this "constant continuity" occurs "the unobstructed and fluid transition of value from one form into the other." That is, value was in a state of unending transformation, appearing "at one time as money, at another time as commodity, then again as exchange value, then again as use value." These networks operated on principles that would remain in force through numerous technological materializations, up to the present. They were not simply neutral high-speed conduits; rather, they were alchemical instruments for generating the abstractions integral to capitalism, which was necessarily destined to be global. Not just manufactured goods but languages, images, forms of social exchange were all to be remade to ensure their compatibility with these systems. It was hardly to be a one-time transmutation, for with each successive upgrading and expansion of these networks, new forms of fluidity and convertibility emerged.

But for the next century and a half (roughly from the 1850s to the 1990s) the metamorphoses and accelerations of an always globalizing capitalism only slowly and partially impose themselves on social and individual life. Modernity, contrary to its popular connotations, is not the world in a sweepingly transformed state. Rather, as some critics have shown, it is the hybrid and dissonant experience of living intermittently within modernized spaces and speeds, and yet simultaneously inhabiting the remnants of pre-capitalist life-worlds, whether social or natural. Wright of Derby's image is an early revelation of modernity's concurrence and contiguity of ultimately incompatible systems. Factory manufacturing, for example, did not abruptly extinguish the long-standing diurnal rhythms and social ties of agrarian milieus. Instead there was an extended period of coexistence during which rural life was incrementally dismantled or subsumed into new processes. There are endless instances of the durability, even if broken and impaired, of older forms, values, techniques, and hierarchies within capitalist modernization. Fredric Jameson suggests that, even by the early twentieth century, "only a minute percentage of the social and physical space of the West could be considered either fully modern in technology or production or substantially bourgeois in its class culture. These twin developments were not completed in most European countries until the end of World War II."[4]

While one might debate the pervasiveness of modernization at various points in time, Jameson's periodization reminds us that the nineteenth century and a good part of the twentieth were effectively a patchwork of disjunct spaces and times, some rationalized and shaped by new institutional and market-based requirements, while in many others premodern patterns and assumptions obdurately survived. Especially significant is the provisional designation of 1945 to indicate a historical turning point. On the mundane level of historical specificity this means recalling, for example, that the Nazis, while developing their V-2 rockets, simultaneously depended on 1.5 million horses for essential military transport.[5] So much for the truism of twentieth-century "mechanized warfare." More importantly, as writers from Ernest Mandel to Thomas Pynchon have shown, World War II, in its destructiveness and global impact, was an unprecedented event of homogenization in which outdated territories, identities, and social fabrics were obliterated. It was the making, wherever possible, of a tabula rasa that would become the platform for the latest phase in the globalization of capitalism. World War II was the crucible in which new paradigms of communication, information, and control were forged, and in which connections between scientific research, transnational corporations, and military power were consolidated.

During the century and a half preceding World War II, one of the ways in which the disparate texture of incomplete or partial modernization can be mapped is through Foucault's account of disciplinary institutions. As he notes, one of the central problems confronting post-revolutionary states and other powerful interests at the start of the nineteenth century was the control and management of potentially unruly populations that had been torn out of premodern milieus and patterns of labor. A technology of power emerges that introduced dispersed methods of regulating the behavior of large numbers of people—in factories, schools, prisons, modern armies, and later in the office spaces of proliferating bureaucracies. Especially in the second half of the nineteenth century and

67

into the twentieth, these were places where individuals were literally confined for long portions of the day or week (or much longer, in the case of prisons) and subjected to an array of mandatory routines and procedures. They were also sites of training, of normalization, and of the accumulation of knowledge about those confined or employed.

But in spite of Foucault's description of disciplinary institutions as a "carceral continuum" blanketing society as a whole, one key element of the historical period in question is the parallel existence of times and places that are unregulated, unorganized, and unsupervised. The problematic notion of everyday life, elusive though it may be, is a valuable overarching way to characterize the shifting and imprecise aggregate of times, behaviors, and sites that effectively constituted layers of *unadministered* life, life at least partially detached from disciplinary imperatives. Even if one attributes a *longue durée* historical status to everyday life, imagining it as an a priori underpinning of all human societies, it should nonetheless be obvious that its possibility and actuality are dramatically transformed by the rise of capitalism. Its material foundations undergo rapid metamorphoses, driven by economic specialization and the privatization of individual experience. However, even amid such changes, everyday life is the repository onto which abiding rudiments of premodern experience, including sleep, are relocated.

For Henri Lefebvre, repetition and habit had always been essential characteristics of the everyday. It was inseparable from cyclical forms of repetition, of days and nights, seasons

and harvests, work and festival, waking and sleeping, creaturely needs and their fulfillment. Even as the actual textures
of agrarian society were steadily eradicated, everyday life stub-
bornly retained, in its structure, some of the invisible
recurring pulsings of life being lived. Many of the consequences of capitalist modernization, as they took shape in the
nineteenth and early twentieth century, seemed antithetical
to the everyday in that they were fundamentally accumula-
tive, anti-cyclical, and developmental, and also brought with
them programmed forms of habit and repetition. There is a
volatile and blurred interplay between the mundane layers of
the everyday that have endured since premodernity and the
gradual insinuation of institutionally generated forms of
routine and monotony that contaminate or displace experiences with links to older patterns. The social and dialogical
milieus of the fair or marketplace are displaced by shopping,
the periodic occurrence of festival is replaced by commodified leisure time, and an endless sequence of specious needs
are fabricated to debase and humiliate the simple acts of sharing through which human appetites had long been gratified
or fulfilled. One of the values of Lefebvre's work is its refusal
of an overtly antagonistic relation between modernity and the
everyday. The everyday is at once too fugitive, too uncircum-
scribed to be imagined as a field of counter-practices to the
codes and institutions of modernization. Even though, at
various points in history, the everyday has been the terrain
from which forms of opposition and resistance may have
come, it is also in the nature of the everyday to adapt and

reshape itself, often submissively, in response to what erupts or intrudes in it. Some have asserted that its passivity has also been its historical resilience, but over the last two decades this belief has been more difficult to sustain.

In the late 1940s and 1950s, the idea of everyday life was a way of describing what was left over, or what remained in the face of economic modernization and the increasing subdivision of social activity. The everyday was the vague constellation of spaces and times *outside* what was organized and institutionalized around work, conformity, and consumerism. It was all the daily habits that were beneath notice, where one remained anonymous. Because it evaded capture and could not be made useful, it was seen by some to have a core of revolutionary potential. For Maurice Blanchot, its dangerous essence was that it was without event, and was both unconcealed and unperceived. In French, the adjective "quotidienne" evokes more strikingly the ancient practice of marking and numbering the passing of the solar day, and it emphasizes the diurnal rhythms that were long a foundation of social existence. But what Lefebvre, Debord, and others also described in the 1950s was the intensifying occupation of everyday life by consumption, organized leisure, and spectacle. In this framework, the rebellions of the late 1960s were, at least in Europe and North America, waged in part around the idea of reclaiming the terrain of everyday life from institutionalization and specialization.

However, with the counter-revolution of the 1980s and the rise of neoliberalism, the marketing of the personal computer, and the dismantling of systems of social protection, the assault on everyday life assumed a new ferocity. Time itself became monetized, and the individual redefined as a full-time economic agent, even in the context of "jobless capitalism."

In a brief but influential text from 1990, Gilles Deleuze proposed that the notion of disciplinary society was no longer an adequate model for explaining contemporary operations of power.[6] He outlined the emergence of what he called "societies of control," in which the institutional regulation of individual and social life proceeded in ways that were continuous and unbounded, and which effectively operated 24/7. He argued that, in disciplinary society, forms of coercion and surveillance occurred within specific sites—the school, the workplace, and the family home—but when occupying the spaces between these sites one was relatively unmonitored. It is possible to identify these various intervals and unregulated spaces as assorted components of everyday life. But a control society, according to Deleuze, was characterized by the disappearance of gaps, of open spaces and times. Mechanisms of command and effects of normalization penetrated almost everywhere and at all times, and they became internalized in a more comprehensive, micrological way than the disciplinary power of the nineteenth and much of the twentieth century. He leaves no doubt that the emergence of this regime of control corresponds to transformations in the world-system of capitalism, to the shift from production to financialization. He also states that any recent technological transformations are only symptomatic, that they are a manifestation of "a mutation in capitalism."

71

As influential as Deleuze's text became, it is clear with hindsight that disciplinary forms of power did not disappear or become superseded, as he maintains. Rather, the continuous forms of control he identifies took shape as an additional layer of regulation alongside still functioning and even amplified forms of discipline. *Contra* Deleuze, the use of harsh physical confinement is greater today than at any time previously, in an expanding network of deliriously panoptic prisons. His evocation of open, amorphous spaces without boundaries is belied by the brutal deployment of walled borders and closed frontiers, both of which strategically target specific populations and regions. Also retrospectively, it can be noted that Deleuze did not address the intensifying overlap between control society and consumer society's proliferating manufacture of individual needs, far beyond the products and commodities that were obligatory even in the 1970s. Nonetheless, in affluent sectors of the globe, what was once consumerism has expanded to 24/7 activity of techniques of personalization, of individuation, of machinic interface, and of mandatory communication. Self-fashioning is the work we are all given, and we dutifully comply with the prescription continually to reinvent ourselves and manage our intricate identities. As Zygmunt Bauman has intimated, we may not grasp that to decline this endless work is not an option.[7]

In a small book by Guy Debord published a year and a half prior to Deleuze's essay, one finds some strikingly similar conclusions. In his *Comments on the Society of the Spectacle*, Debord identifies a new intensity and comprehensiveness with which individual existence has been penetrated by effects of domination. He is not proposing a paradigm shift of the sort suggested by Deleuze, but rather indicating that there has been a modification in the nature of spectacle, a move from the *diffuse* spectacle of the 1960s (the label he used to characterize consumer societies in the West) to what he sees as a global *integrated* spectacle. The key difference is that in the 1960s there were still areas of social life that remained relatively autonomous and exempt from effects of spectacle, while at the time he is writing (around 1990), there are none. Everyday life is no longer politically relevant, and it endures only as a hollowed-out simulation of its former substantiality. "Beyond a legacy of old books and old buildings . . . there remains nothing, in culture or in nature, which has not been transformed and polluted, according to the means and interests of modern industry."[8]

At the time, Debord and Deleuze were writing against the grain. The "short twentieth century" was coming to an abrupt end, between 1989 and 1991, with what to many seemed like hopeful developments, including the fall of the Berlin Wall and the dissolution of a bipolar, Cold War world. Along with the triumphalist narratives of globalization and the facile declarations of the historical end of competing world-systems were the widely promoted "paradigms" for a post-political and post-ideological era. Twenty years later, it is difficult to recall the seriousness with which these fatuous claims were made on behalf of a West that seemed poised to effortlessly occupy and refashion the entire planet. Not by accident, this was also the moment when the vague entity then magically evoked as cyberspace appeared, seemingly out of nowhere. It was heralded as an unprecedented set of tools with nothing less than the power to reinvent the self and its relation to the world. But even by the mid 1990s, the promotional retro-psychedelic euphoria had vanished, as it became clearer that though cyberspace was, in fact, a reinvention of the self, it was transnational corporations doing the reinventing and transforming.

But that moment of the early 1990s was decisive less for anything novel or unprecedented than for the fulfillment and consolidation of systemic possibilities that were incipient in Arkwright's mills, and which became only partially realized with the transportation and communication networks of the nineteenth century. By the end of the twentieth century it had become possible to see a broader and much fuller integration of the human subject with the "constant continuity" of a 24/7 capitalism that had always been inherently global. Today, the permanently operating domains of communication and of the production and circulation of information penetrate everywhere. A temporal alignment of the individual with the functioning of markets, two centuries in developing, has made irrelevant distinctions between work and non-work time, between public and private, between everyday life and organized institutional milieus. Under these conditions, the relentless financialization of previously autonomous spheres of social activity continues unchecked. Sleep is the only remaining barrier, the only enduring "natural condition" that capitalism cannot eliminate.

In the late 1990s, when Google was barely a one-year-old privately-held company, its future CEO was already articulating the context in which such a venture would flourish. Dr. Eric Schmidt declared that the twenty-first century would be synonymous with what he called the "attention economy," and that the dominant global corporations would be those that succeed in maximizing the number of "eyeballs" they could consistently engage and control.[9] The intensity of the competition for access to or control of an individual's waking hours each day is a result of the vast disproportion between those human, temporal limits and the quasi-infinite amount of "content" being marketed. But corporate success will also be measured by the amount of information that can be extracted, accumulated, and used to predict and modify the behavior of any individual with a digital identity. One of the goals of Google, Facebook, and other enterprises (five years from now the names may be different) is to normalize and make indispensable, as Deleuze outlined, the idea of a continuous interface—not literally seamless, but a relatively unbroken engagement with illuminated screens of diverse kinds that unremittingly demand interest or response. Of course, there are breaks, but they are not intervals in which any kind of counter-projects or streams of thought can be nurtured and sustained. As the opportunity for electronic transactions of all kinds becomes omnipresent, there is no vestige of what used to be everyday life beyond the reach of corporate intrusion. An attention economy dissolves the separation between the personal and professional, between entertainment and information, all overridden by a compulsory functionality of communication that is inherently and inescapably 24/7. Even as a contemporary colloquialism, the term "eyeballs" for the site of control repositions human vision as a *motor* activity that can be subjected to external direction or stimuli. The goal is to refine the capacity to localize the eye's movement on or within highly targeted sites or points of interest. The eye is dislodged from the realm of optics and made into an intermediary element of a circuit whose end result is always a motor response of the body to electronic solicitation. It is out of this context that Google and other corporate players now compete for dominance over the remains of the everyday. Some will argue that what constitutes everyday life is continually recreating itself, and that today it is flourishing in specific areas of online exchange and expression. However, if one accepts that a meaningful notion of everyday life is inseparable from its fugitive anonymity, then it would be difficult to grasp what it might have in common with time spent in which one's gestures are all recorded, permanently archived, and processed with the aim of predetermining one's future choices and actions.

There is a well-known critical tradition, going back to the late nineteenth century, which identifies the standardization of experience as one of the defining attributes of Western modernity. Initially, the idea of routinization was drawn from the industrial workplace and its requirement of the continuous performance of repetitive actions and tasks. At the start of the twentieth century, the notion was expanded to include crucial aspects of emerging mass societies, such as the uniformity of state and corporate bureaucracies and the impact of mass-produced goods within a modern culture of consumption. However, for much of the previous century, the spheres of work and of leisure, of the public and the personal, had maintained, in appearance or reality, some degree of distinctness and separation. Despite the often oppressive routinization and habit, life for many was a differentiated texture of variegated routines that were woven in and out of at least some unregulated spaces and times. Habit, in this sense, is a way of understanding actual social behavior as located somewhere between the imagined extremes of a manipulated society of sleepers and a mobilized nation of "awakened" individuals. Of course, in discussing the nineteenth and twentieth centuries, I am referring to several unique and specific historical phenomena as well as to the habits they produced: for example, the many strategies for mechanizing and rationalizing human activity in work environments and the standardization of many forms of cultural consumption. Part of my larger argument is that important convergences of these areas have been a crucial part of neoliberal initiatives since the 1980s. The result is the emergence of forms of habit that are inevitably 24/7 and reciprocally tied to mechanisms of power that are equally "continuous and unbounded."

In the early 1900s, the problem of habit within modernity was troubling for many philosophers and social theorists who believed in participatory democracy. Of these, John Dewey is one of the best known, in particular for his concern that forms of automatic, habitual behavior accompanying industrial modernity clashed with the possibility of an intelligent and reflective citizenry on whom a democratic politics depended. However, Dewey's way out of this impasse was to insist, with his characteristic optimism, that habit in its modern guises could produce its own overcoming. Novelty and communication, he argued, would inevitably discourage repetitive patterns. "Each habit demands appropriate conditions for its exercise and when habits are numerous and complex, as with the human organism, to find these conditions involves search and experimentation . . . By a seeming paradox, increased power of forming habits means increased susceptibility, sensitiveness, responsiveness."[10] Dewey's deep understanding of the social nature of habit had convinced him that a society was defined, in essential ways, by the habits out of which it was composed, and clearly this was one reason why the reform of early education was of such importance to him; he believed that "intelligent" or collectively beneficial habits could be nurtured pedagogically. But Dewey, born in 1859 (the same year as Henri Bergson, who shared many of these concerns), was part of a generation whose intellectual formation occurred when it was still possible, if not excusable, for the idea of novelty to be explored independently of the logistics of capitalist production and circulation. In the mid twentieth century, it would have been more difficult for him, or others, to evade how the new was effectively inseparable from its monotonous reproduction in the service of the present against any truly different future. By the 1950s, the production of novelty, in all its dispiriting

forms, had become a central enterprise of advanced econo-
mies all over the globe.

When Dewey died in 1952, aged ninety-three, the manufacture of new forms of habit had begun to include some essential
elements of what would become the 24/7 control society
outlined by Deleuze, or the integrated spectacle of Debord.
Just as the nighttime lighting in Arkwright's factories was an
early hint of future alignments of lived temporalities with
market needs, so the mass diffusion of television in the 1950s
was another turning point in the market's appropriation of
previously unannexed times and spaces. One can imagine a
pairing of Wright's painting, each of its factory windows illuminated by the oil lamps that allowed work to proceed
continuously, with a mid-twentieth-century image of a not
dissimilar multi-story building with windows lit by the glow of
television sets. In both cases, there is a transformational relation between a deployment of light sources and the social
construction of time. The cathode ray tube was a decisive and
vivid instance of how the glare and gossip of a public transac-
tional world penetrated the most private of spaces, and
contaminated the quiet and solitude that Arendt believed
essential for the sustenance of a political individual. Television
quickly redefined what constituted membership in society.
Even the pretense of valuing education and civic participation
dwindled, as citizenship was supplanted by viewership.

One of the many innovations of television was its imposition
of homogeneous and habitual behaviors on spheres of life that
had previously been subject to less direct forms of control. At

the same time, it was the setting in place of conditions which would subsequently be essential for the 24/7 "attention economy" of the twenty-first century. Appearing amid the delayed shocks of World War II, television was the site of a destabilization of relations between exposure and protectedness, agency and passivity, sleep and waking, and publicness and privacy. Because of the pervasive need for a semblance of continuity and social cohesion in the aftermath of Hiroshima and Auschwitz, the radical disruptiveness of television was generally overlooked. Instead, normalcy and coherence were attributed to this new televisual world beheld in common, in which anything could be coupled with anything whatever. It was the omnipresent antidote to shock. Much more decisively than radio, television was a crucial site in which the enormous inequality of scale between global systems and the local, circumscribed lives of individuals became quickly naturalized.

The relatively sudden and ubiquitous reorganization of human time and activity accompanying television had little historical precedent. Cinema and radio were only partial anticipations of the structural changes it introduced. Within the space of barely fifteen years, there was a mass relocation of populations into extended states of relative immobilization. Hundreds of millions of individuals precipitously began spending many hours of every day and night sitting, more or less stationary, in close proximity to flickering, light-emitting objects. All of the myriad ways in which time had been spent, used, squandered, endured, or parcellized prior to television time were replaced by more uniform modes of duration and a narrowing of sensory responsiveness. Television brought equally significant changes to an external social world and to an interior psychic landscape, scrambling the relations between these two poles. It involved an immense displacement of human praxis to a far more circumscribed and unvarying range of relative inactivity.

As many critics have shown, television is hardly an autonomous technological invention. Its scientific and mechanical premises were available to engineers in the 1920s, yet it took on its post–World War II forms only in the context of a commodity-based and US-dominated global economy, and of a new demographic mobility in patterns of daily life.[11] As disciplinary norms in the workplace and in schools lost their effectiveness, television was crafted into a machinery of regulation, introducing previously unknown effects of subjection and supervision. This is why television is a crucial and adaptable part of a relatively long transition (or changing of the guard), lasting several decades, between a world of older disciplinary institutions and one of 24/7 control. It could be argued that, during the 1950s and '60s, television introduced into the home disciplinary strategies modeled elsewhere. In spite of more uprooted and transient lifestyles following the war, television's effects were anti-nomadic: individuals are fixed in place, partitioned from one another, and emptied of political effectiveness. At least partially, this corresponds to an industrial model of being set to work. Although no physical labor occurs, it is an arrangement in which the management of individuals overlaps with the production of surplus value, since new accumulation was driven by the size of television audiences.

In retrospect, during this period of twenty years, perhaps longer, from the early 1950s into the 1970s, television in North America was remarkably stable as a system, with a small number of channels and durable programming formats, and without a continual stream of competing technological products. Networks had their offerings conform to traditional sleep patterns of human beings, with their nightly sign-offs— although in retrospect the after-midnight test-pattern seems like a placeholder for the inevitable 24/7 transmissions soon to come. Whether this phase corresponded to post-war American world hegemony and to the monopolistic framework of the broadcasting industry has long been debated. By the late 1970s, perhaps earlier, the word "television" conveyed and encompassed far more than the objects and networks literally denoted. Television became a nebulous but loaded figure for evoking the texture of modernity and a transformed everyday life. The word concretized, in something localizable, broader experiences of de-realization. It alluded to the decay of a more palpable immediate world and to how the spectral dislocations of modernization had been normalized as a familiar presence in the most intimate aspects of our lives. Television incarnated the falseness of the world, but it also eliminated any position from which a "true" world could be imagined. It demonstrated effects of power that could not be explained within the familiar poles of coercive and non-coercive, despite the many characterizations of television as an instrument of behavioral control, from "influencing machine" to "image-virus." Instead of a tele-vision-saturated culture diminishing individual agency, its pervasiveness made clear that agency itself is a mutable and historically determined notion.

This post-war era of television was clearly over by the mid 1980s. Even as early as 1983, the wide availability of the VCR and the standardization of VHS, video-game consoles, and fully commercialized cable TV significantly altered the positions and capabilities of what had been television up to then. In the middle of the 1980s the marketing of the personal computer had begun, and by the early 1990s this ubiquitous product would symbolically announce the advent of a society of control after an extended transitional phase. The 1980s are often characterized as a period during which there was an abandonment of the merely receptive or passive role of the original television viewer. In its place, according to this version, emerged a more creative user of a far larger field of media resources, who was able to intervene purposively in the utilization of technological products, and by the early 1990s able to interface with global information networks. The interactive possibilities of these new tools were touted as empowering, and as intrinsically democratic and anti-hierar-chical—although much of the force of these myths has since been deflated. What was celebrated as interactivity was more accurately the mobilization and habituation of the individual to an open-ended set of tasks and routines, far beyond what was asked of anyone in the 1950s and '60s. Television had colonized important arenas of lived time, but neoliberalism demanded that there be a far more methodical extraction of value from television time, and in principle from every waking hour. In this sense 24/7 capitalism is not simply a continuous or sequential capture of attention, but also a dense layering of time, in which multiple operations or attractions can be attended to in near-simultaneity, regardless of where one is or whatever else one might be doing. So-called "smart" devices are labeled as such less for the advantages they might provide for an individual than for their capacity to integrate their user more fully into 24/7 routines.

However, it would be misguided to suggest that there was ever a complete break with the supposedly passive and receptive model of television. A tendency in recent media theory has been to qualify or suspend the language of rupture or discontinuity in discussing the relations between "old" media and "new" digital technologies. Instead, older models and arrangements are understood to persist in various forms of hybridity, convergence, remediation, or recuperation. Regardless of what specific theoretical explanation is used, it is clear that television, or at least crucial elements of what it used to be, have been amalgamated into new services, networks, and devices in which its capabilities and effects are continually modified. Nonetheless, as recent statistics on viewing habits indicate, a significant chunk of our current 24/7 world is filled with the televisual. Nielsen numbers for 2010 show that the average American consumed video content of various kinds for approximately five hours a day. Some of those hours coincide with other activities and apparatuses, just as one's relation to video now entails a range of managerial tasks and options, as discussed in the previous chapter. Nonetheless, it is important to acknowledge, even if it cannot be quantified, the persistence and durability of some of the original conditions that defined television's relation to a perceiver.

In 2006, researchers at Cornell University released results of a long-term study containing some hypotheses about the reorganization of television in the 1980s. The research project assembled data to suggest a correlation between television viewing by very young children and autism.[12] One of the most urgent problems in autism studies has been to explain the extraordinary and anomalous rise in its frequency beginning in the mid to late 1980s. From the late 1970s, when autism occurred in one out of 2,500 children, the rate of incidence has risen so fast that, as of a few years ago, it affected approximately one in 150 children, and showed no sign of leveling off. Genetic predisposition, enlarged diagnostic criteria, prenatal events, infections, parental age, vaccines, and other environmental factors have all been proposed as possible factors. The Cornell project was unusual in its expansion of "environmental" to include something as universal and apparently innocuous as a television set. Obviously, television had been pervasive in North American homes since the 1950s: Why then might it have markedly different consequences beginning in the 1980s? The study proposes that a new coalescence of factors occurred in that decade—in particular, the widespread availability of cable TV, the growth of dedicated children's channels and video cassettes, and the popularity of VCRs, as well as huge increases in households with two or more television sets. Thus conditions were, and continue to be, in place for the exposure of very young children to television for extended periods of time on a daily basis. Their specific conclusions were relatively cautious: that extended television viewing before the age of three can trigger the onset of the disorder in "at risk" children.

The broader implications of this study were unacceptable to many, and it was the object of attacks and official ridicule. It made the heretical suggestion that television might have a catastrophic *physical* impact on the developing human being—that it could produce extreme, permanent impairments in the acquisition of language and in the capacity for social interaction. It more than hinted at the transformation of what had been *metaphoric* characterizations of television as a communicative pathology into real effects and consequences. Regardless of what future research may prove or disprove concerning a link between television and autism, the Cornell study foregrounded crucial experiential features of the apparatus. For one, it indicated the obvious: that in growing numbers, television and screens of many kinds are becoming part of the waking environment of younger and younger children. More importantly, it bypassed the notion that television is something one *watches* in some attentive manner, and instead provisionally treated it as a source of light and sound to which one is *exposed*. Given the fragility and vulnerability of very young children who were the object of the study, it means reconsidering exposure in terms of lasting physical damage to the nervous system.

Television, as Raymond Williams and others showed, never simply involved choosing to watch discrete programs, but was a more promiscuous interface with a stream of luminous stimulation, albeit with diverse kinds of narrative content.[13] The precise nature of the physiological attraction of television has yet to be specified, and may never be, but a huge amount of statistical and anecdotal evidence obviously has confirmed the truism that it has potent addictive properties. However, television posed the unusual phenomenon of an addictiveness to something that failed to deliver the most basic reward of a habit-forming substance: that is, it provides not even a temporary heightened sense of well-being or pleasure, or a gratifying if brief fall into insensate numbness. Moments after turning on a television, there is no detectable rush or charge of sensation of any kind. Rather, there is a slow shift into a vacancy from which one finds it difficult to disengage. This is a decisive trait of the era of technological addictiveness: that one can return again and again to a neutral void that has little affective intensity of any kind. In the widely noted study by Kubey and Csikszentmihalyi, the majority of their subjects reported that extended TV viewing made them feel worse than when they did not watch, yet they felt compelled to continue their behavior.[14] The longer they watched, the worse they felt. The hundreds of studies on depression and internet use show similar kinds of results. Even the quasi-addictiveness associated with internet pornography and violent computer games seems to lead quickly to a flattening of response and the replacement of pleasure with the need for repetition.

Television was only the first of a category of apparatuses with which we are currently surrounded that are most often used out of powerful habitual patterning involving a diffuse attentiveness and a semi-automatism. In this sense, they are part of larger strategies of power in which the aim is not mass-deception, but rather states of neutralization and inactivation, in which one is dispossessed of time. But even within habitual repetitions there remains a thread of hope—a knowingly false hope—that one more click or touch might open onto something to redeem the overwhelming monotony in which one is immersed. One of the forms of disempowerment within 24/7 environments is the incapacitation of daydream or of any mode of absent-minded introspection that would otherwise occur in intervals of slow or vacant time. Now one of the attractions of current systems and products is their operating speed: it has become intolerable for there to be waiting time while something loads or connects. When there are delays or breaks of empty time, they are rarely openings for the drift of consciousness in which one becomes unmoored from the constraints and demands of the immediate present. There is a profound incompatibility of anything resembling reverie with the priorities of efficiency, functionality, and speed.

There are of course numerous interruptions to the 24/7 seizure of attentiveness. Beginning with television, but especially in the last two decades, one became familiar with the transitional moments when one shuts off an apparatus after having been immersed in any televisual or digital ambience for an extended period. There is inevitably a brief interval *before* the world fully recomposes itself into its unthought and unseen familiarity. It is an instant of disorientation when one's immediate surroundings—for example, a room and its contents—seem both vague and oppressive in their time-worn materiality, their heaviness, their vulnerability to dilapidation, but also their inflexible resistance to being clicked away in an instant. One has a fleeting intuition of the disparity between one's sense of limitless electronic connectedness and the enduring constraints of embodiment and physical finitude. But such dislocating moments were generally restricted to the physical sites in which non-portable apparatuses were available. With increasingly prosthetic devices, these kinds of transitions occur anywhere, in every conceivable public or private milieu. Experience now consists of sudden and frequent shifts from absorption in a cocoon of control and personalization into the contingency of a shared world intrinsically resistant to control. The experience of these shifts inevitably enhances one's attraction to the former, and magnifies the mirage of one's own privileged exemption from the apparent shoddiness and insufficiency of a world in common. Within 24/7 capitalism, a sociality outside of individual self-interest becomes inexorably depleted, and the interhuman basis of public space is made irrelevant to one's fantasmatic digital insularity.

CHAPTER FOUR

Chris Marker's *La jetée* (1962) opens in a post-apocalyptic future where surviving humans inhabit cramped underground spaces beneath destroyed cities in permanent exile from daylight. The authorities in this near future are desperately experimenting with primitive forms of time travel to locate help for their beleaguered existence. Part of the crisis is the deterioration and failure of memory in all but a few individuals. The protagonist, and subject of the experiments, has been chosen for the tenaciousness with which he has been able to retain an image from the past. Clearly, *La jetée* is not a story of the future but a meditation on the present, in this case the early 1960s, which Marker portrays as a dark time, shadowed by the death camps, the devastation of Hiroshima, and torture in Algeria. Like contemporary work by Alain Resnais (*Hiroshima, mon amour*), Jacques Rivette (*Paris nous appartient*), Joseph Losey (*These Are the Damned*), Fritz Lang (*Die Tausend Augen des Dr*

Mabuse), Jacques Tourneur (*The Fearmakers*), and numerous others, the film seems to ask: How does one remain human in the bleakness of this world when the ties that connect us have been shattered and when malevolent forms of rationality are powerfully at work? Although Marker's answer to such a question remains unspecified, *La jetée* affirms the indispensability of the imagination for collective survival. For Marker, this implies a mingling of the visionary capacities of both memory and creation, and it occurs in the film around the image of the unsighted, blindfolded protagonist. Although most of the film, in its narrative context, consists of remembered or imagined images, one of its original premises is this model of a seer whose normative visual abilities have been deactivated in circumstances evoking the torture and inhumane medical experiments of the war and in the years that followed.

Marker here departs from understandings of "inner" vision that presuppose the autonomy and self-sufficiency of a *voyant*. In *La jetée* the seer's subjective freedom is constrained, even partly directed, by the external compulsion of his circumstances, and his extraordinary recovery (or creation) of mental images occurs in an ambiguous overlap of scarcity and fear, on one hand, and the marvelous flux of a "vie intérieure" on the other. Marker is clearly familiar with previous explorations of reverie and daydream (from Rousseau to Nerval, Proust, Bachelard, and others), but the reverie of *La jetée*'s protagonist is not simply an aleatory suspension of self in a stream of consciousness. Instead, his drift between images is always counterbalanced by the exigencies of a doomed present, by the anxiety of a state of emergency, and by the application of biopower to compel his mnemonic cooperation. Marker may well be alluding to the Surrealist poet Robert Desnos, known for his ability to fall into deep trance-like sleeps, during which he uttered verbal outpourings of dream imagery. The mediumistic Desnos, who hosted a popular radio program on dreams in the 1930s, was condemned to a situation not unlike that depicted in the opening of *La jetée*: he was deported to Auschwitz in 1944, transferred to other camps, and died of typhus days after the war's end.

Much of the richness of Marker's film stems from its distancing of photography from empirical notions of reality or indexical models of this medium. An image is "real" affectively, in how it feels, in how it verifies the intensity of a lived or remembered moment. For example, when the protagonist has his first recollections (or dreams) of the past, there is no equivocation concerning the ontological status of these internally generated images: they are "real" birds, "real" children, seemingly more authentic than his underground prison surroundings. Marker is working at a moment when, in France and elsewhere, there is a growing sense of the deadening effects of a standardized and image-saturated culture. In resisting the constraints and technical administration of the present, *La jetée* poses the extreme difficulty and exhilaration of its central vocation: "to imagine or dream another time." Marker advances the necessity of such a visionary project, but also discloses its tenuousness and perhaps inevitable failure. But for the 1960s just beginning, and for the generation to come, he situated a utopian moment, not in the future yet to be made but in the imbrication of memory and the present, in the lived inseparability of sleep and waking, of dream and life, in a dream of life as the inextinguishable promise of awakening.

The most celebrated moment in *La jetée* occurs when the sequential stasis of still photographs is briefly supplanted by the cinematic illusion of human eyes opening, as if out of sleep. This appearance of animated life (also created out of static images) seems an indirect response to Hitchcock's *Psycho* (1960). In this film from two years earlier, Marker would have seen Hitchcock's shot of Janet Leigh, following the shower murder, sprawled on the bathroom floor with eyes open. One's impression, even after many viewings, is that a still photograph has been used to convey the stillness of a corpse—that an actor would have been unable so completely to suppress all the motility and quavering musculature of eyes and face for a take of over twenty-five seconds. Before the camera cuts away, a drop of water falls across her hair, abruptly demonstrating that the motionless, open-eyed face has been shown in "real time," corresponding to the sound of the running shower. In Laura Mulvey's superb analysis of this sequence, she raises questions that are relevant to *La jetée* as well: "The paradox of the cinema's uncertain boundary between stillness and movement also finds a fleeting visibility. The stillness of the corpse is a reminder that the cinema's living and moving bodies are simply animate stills and the homology between stillness and death returns to haunt the moving image."[1] But linking Marker and Hitchcock here is the manner in which their particular engagement with the static basis of cinematic movement are part of broader insights into the texture of contemporary social experience.

Both *La jetée* and *Psycho*, in the early 1960s, reveal how the remaking or congealing of life into things or images disrupts the framework of a historical time in which change can occur. The darkness of *Psycho* is of a present in which a pathological attempt to freeze time and identities collides disastrously with the rootlessness and anonymity of modernity. Hitchcock's amalgam of ancestral home and roadside motel encapsulates two intertwined components of mid-twentieth-century experience. In the old Bates house, all the traditional identifications with place, family, and continuity have deteriorated into a morbid resistance to any alteration of an imaginary domestic matrix. Time, development, and maturation have been arrested into a museum-like space, amplified by Norman's recourse to taxidermy. Taxidermy, invented in the 1820s, has been described as one instance of a "resurrection" paradigm in which various techniques produce the illusion of life out of what is dead or inert.[2] Taxidermy is present in both *Psycho* and *La jetée* as a "reality effect" that is continuous with the operation of both cinematic and photographic illusion.

But if Norman is the proprietor-curator of the "historically preserved" house on the hill, he is also the operator of that key emblem of modern placelessness and mobility, the motel. In its run-down anonymity, the motel stands on a depthless, lateral terrain of flux and exchangeability, of temporary and provisional life, nourished only by the circulation of money whose main purpose is to "buy off unhappiness." The vertical layering of the petrified family house and the horizontal drift of the motel–highway–used car lot network are interdependent parts of a broken and increasingly inanimate world. The opening words of the ciné-roman *La jetée* bespeak its thematic proximity to a crucial element of the *Psycho* backstory: "This is the story of a man marked by an image from his childhood, by the violent scene which upset him . . . " Nonetheless, Marker's configuring of memory, time, and image indicated his affiliation with a very different intellectual heritage, remote from Hitchcock's own ambivalence about desire. What the self takes to be memory may be damaged or partial, but like the ruined statues in the museum visit in *La jetée*, it contains at least possible pathways toward individual freedom. Even the taxidermy in Marker's film—whales and other mammals in a natural history display—is not a disturbing *nature morte* but a glimpse of timelessness in the present. The objects are not a symbolic form of survival in the face of time's destructiveness, but an apprehension of the marvelous, of a real that is outside of a life/death or waking/dream duality.

But the avenues of flight in *La jetée* are menaced by institutional powers who instrumentalize the protagonist into a temporarily useful object who is then relegated to the status of a disposable thing. In reductive terms, the narrative elements of Marker's film can be linked to a significant number of science fiction scenarios, beginning in the mid 1950s, in which dreams or memories are presented as phenomena accessible to outside examination or intervention. (In *La jetée*: "The camp police spied even on dreams.") But over the last decade or more, what was generally restricted to the speculative confines of a popular fiction genre has now become part of a mass imagination, nourished and reinforced by many sources. In basic form, it is the pervasive assumption that dreams are objectifiable, that they are discrete entities that, given the development of applicable technology, could be recorded and in some way played back or downloaded. During the last few years, news stories have sensationally heralded research at UC Berkeley and Berlin's Max Planck Institute for using data from brain scans of visual cortex activity in dreaming subjects to generate digital images that allegedly represent what the subjects are dreaming of. Big-budget movies such as Christopher Nolan's *Inception* amplify the notion that dreams are effectively a product that can be used and manipulated like other kinds of media content. The currency of such fantasies is enhanced by the announcement of related developments in brain research: for example, the assertion that brain scanners at airports and elsewhere soon will be able to detect "pernicious thoughts" in potential terrorists.

The manifest unlikelihood, or absurdity, of such possibilities ever being realized is less important than how they are shaping and regulating contemporary imaginaries. There is a broad remodeling of the dream into something like media software or a kind of "content" to which, in principle, there could be instrumental access. This generalized notion of accessibility derives from elements of popular culture that emerged in the mid 1980s in cyberpunk fiction, but which quickly saturated a broader collective sensibility. In various ways, there was a development of figures for new types of interfaces or circuits in which the mind or nervous system effectively linked up with the operation and flows of external systems. The idea of an actual neural connection to a global grid or matrix was, in most cases, a valorization of heightened states of *exposure*, whether to streams of images, information, or code. One effect of this imposition of an input/output model is a homogenization of inner experience and the contents of communication networks, and an unproblematic reduction of the infinite amorphousness of mental life to digital formats. Richard K. Morgan's novel *Altered Carbon* (2002) can stand for a large category of current fiction in which individual consciousness can be digitized, downloaded, stored, installed in a new body, and have the ability to interface with boundless reservoirs of data. At the same time, narratives detailing such delirious levels of exposure are usually constructed as fables of empowerment, in spite of the extreme asymmetry between the individual and the inconceivable scale of "the grid." The lesson, in different guises, demonstrates how an entrepreneurial heroism is capable of surmounting this asymmetry and leveraging its incommensurabilities to one's individual benefit. The problem here is not to be construed as the permeability between some undefiled inner life and external techniques and processes. Rather, it is one sign of a larger tendency to reconceive all facets of individual experience as continuous and compatible with the requirements of accelerated 24/7 consumerism. Even though dreaming will always evade such appropriation, it inevitably becomes culturally figured as software or content detachable from the self, as something that might be circulated electronically or posted as an online video.

It is part of a larger set of processes in which everything once considered personal has to be recreated and deployed in the service of adding dollar or prestige value to one's electronic identities.

In spite of the many dismissals it has received over the past few decades, it is obvious how important the concept of reification, or some closely affiliated account, remains for any understanding of global capitalism and technological culture. Whether one's vantage point is Marxist or not, there is no evading the extent to which the internet and digital communications have been the engine of the relentless financialization and commodification of more and more regions of individual and social life. This has created a field of conditions markedly distinct from several decades ago. As late as the 1960s, numerous critiques of consumer culture outlined the dissonance between an environment saturated by images and products and the individual who, though ensnared in its shallowness and falseness, grasped even dimly its essential discrepancy with their hopes and life needs. One endlessly consumed products that inevitably failed to fulfill their original, if fraudulent, promises. At present, however, the idea of a divergence between a human world and the operation of global systems with the capacity to occupy every waking hour of one's life seems dated and inapt. Now there are numerous pressures for individuals to reimagine and refigure themselves as being of the same consistency and values as the dematerialized commodities and social connections in which they are immersed so extensively. Reification has proceeded to the point where the individual has to invent a self-understanding that optimizes or facilitates their participation in digital milieus and speeds. Paradoxically, this means impersonating the inert and the inanimate. These particular terms might seem deeply unsuited to providing an account of emulation and identification with the shifting and intangible events and processes with which one becomes technologically engaged. Because one cannot literally enter any of the electronic mirages that constitute the interlocking marketplaces of global consumerism, one is obliged to construct fantasmatic compatibilities between the human and a realm of choices that is fundamentally unlivable.

There is no possible harmonization between actual living beings and the demands of 24/7 capitalism, but there are countless inducements to delusionally suspend or obscure some of the humiliating limitations of lived experience, whether emotional or biological. Figurations of the inert or inanimate also operate as a protective or numbing shield, to evade recognition of the harsh expendability of life within contemporary economic and institutional arrangements. There is a pervasive illusion that, as more of the earth's biosphere is annihilated or irreparably damaged, human beings can magically disassociate themselves from it and transfer their interdependencies to the mecanosphere of global capitalism. The more one identifies with the insubstantial electronic surrogates for the physical self, the more one seems to conjure an exemption from the biocide underway everywhere on the planet. At the same time, one becomes chillingly oblivious to the fragility and transience of actual living things.

In the contemporary marketplace, the many products and services that promise to "reverse the aging process" are not appealing to a fear of death so much as offering superficial ways to simulate the non-human properties and temporalities of the digital zones one is already inhabiting for much of each day. Also, the belief that one can subsist independently of environmental catastrophe is paralleled by fantasies of individual survival or prosperity amid the destruction of civil society and the elimination of institutions that retain any semblance of social protection or mutual support, whether public education, social services, or healthcare for those most in need.

This remapping of the experience of reification can be illustrated by reference to the disparity of two related artifacts, one from the 1960s and the other from the 1980s: Philip K. Dick's novel *Do Androids Dream of Electric Sheep?* and the film *Blade Runner*, directed by Ridley Scott. In the near future of Dick's novel, one of the rarest commodities is living animals, as most have become extinct due to environmental collapse and nuclear radiation. Large corporations invest in the small number that remain, and only the very wealthy could ever own one. All any middle-class person can afford is an industrially produced cybernetic animal, identical in most ways to a live one, except that it has no awareness of the existence of a person and no capacity for anything other than programmed responses, remaining at its core an obdurate, insensate thing. Hence the importance in the novel of the regularly published price list of the going rate for any surviving species of live animal (Sidney's Animal & Fowl Catalogue). Dick recounts the moment when the main character sees a live raccoon on display in the offices of a robotics corporation:

> It was not surprise that he felt but more a sort of yearning. He quietly walked away from the girl toward the closest pen. Already he could smell them, the several scents of the creatures standing or sitting, or, in the case of what appeared to be a raccoon, asleep. Never in his life had he personally seen a raccoon. In an automatic response, he brought out his much-thumbed Sidney's and looked up raccoon with all the sublistings. The list prices, naturally, appeared in italics; like Percheron horses, none existed on the market for sale at any figure. Sidney's catalogue simply listed the price at which the last transaction had taken place. It was astronomical.

The price tag itself, the dollar figure, is the locus of an acute longing and emotional emptiness. Even in its abstraction, the cost price becomes the overinvested sign mediating one's sense of wonderment and desire for something living and vulnerable like oneself, something to overcome what Dick calls "the tyranny of the object."

Much of his fiction is a piercing elaboration of the subjective costs of living within a reality undergoing continual cancellation and demolition. He is the preeminent chronicler of a phantasmagoric, commodity-filled world colored by transience and loss. A Dick novel, especially those written between 1964 and 1970, usually follows an individual who in a limited way resists but most often merely struggles to survive the ongoing deterioration of the world. His work is one of the great literary accounts of the psychic costs of reification, of what he calls "a peculiar malign abstractness" within the culture of mid-twentieth-century capitalism. Dick describes a social field that has been repeatedly remade and modernized, but he preserves a sense of the present as stratified and littered with the debris or abject persistence of earlier phases of modernization. In Dick's work we are trapped amid things that are inexorably consigned to a squalid uselessness that insinuates itself as a condition of human experience.

But the refusal to capitulate to the laws of a thing-like existence in *Do Androids Dream?* gives way to something very different in its film adaptation. The novel's account of the unremitting and petty ruin of individual experience is turned into a world-weary celebration of the petrification and "malign abstractness" from which Dick recoiled. Appearing during the early Reagan-Thatcher years, *Blade Runner* is an outline of a reconfigured relationship to an emerging global consumer culture that would be more securely in place by the 1990s. Rather than tracking any kind of split between the self and this milieu, the film affirms a functional assimilation of the individual into the circuitry and workings of an expanded field of commodification. It makes emotionally credible the bleak threshold at which the technological products of corporations become the object of our desires, our hopes. The film visualized the de-differentiated spaces in which machines and humans were interchangeable, in which distinctions between living and inanimate, between human memories and fabricated memory implants, cease to be meaningful. The dystopic disorientation of *Blade Runner* may seem to depict the texture of a fallen world, but there is no longer the recollection available even to care from what it might have fallen.

Several decades later a related de-differentiation pervades most areas of mass technological culture. The fictive figuration of dreams as accessible and objectifiable is merely one part of the background to the unending demand for the externalization of one's life into pre-made digital formats. In a hyper-expansion of the logic of spectacle, there is a reassembling of the self into a new hybrid of consumer and object of consumption. If something as private and seemingly interior as dreaming is now the object of advanced brain scanners and can be imagined in popular culture as downloadable media content, then there are few restraints on the objectification of those parts of individual life that can be more easily relocated to digital formats. Everyone, we are told—not just businesses and institutions—needs an "online presence," needs 24/7 exposure, to avoid social irrelevance or professional failure. But the promotion of these alleged benefits is a cover for the transfer of most social relations into monetized and quantifiable forms. It is equally a shift of individual life to conditions in which privacy is impossible, and in which one becomes a permanent site of data-harvesting and surveillance. One accumulates a patchwork of surrogate identities that subsist 24/7, sleeplessly, continuously, as inanimate impersonations rather than extensions of the self. Inanimate here does not mean the literal absence of motion, but rather a simulated release from the hindrances of being alive which are incompatible with circulation and exchangeability. Sensory impoverishment and the reduction of perception to habit and engineered response is the inevitable result of aligning oneself with the multifarious products, services, and "friends" that one consumes, manages, and accumulates during waking life.

Some of the most basic questions surrounding sleep and dreaming, still relevant today, were asked by Aristotle. He resisted the temptation to pose sleep as a monolithic state that was simply the contrary of waking, because of the fact that experience did not cease for the sleeper. He wanted to know the precise status of the perceptual data designated as dream. To what extent are they imaginative, sensory, or merely physiological processes? Aristotle and his contemporaries, in common with most other premodern societies, made qualitative distinctions between different kinds of dreams—for example, between those that merely seemed to rehash the emotions and events of the recent past and rarer dreams that seemed to have a revelatory or prophetic force. For all the cultural diversity in how dreams were understood from antiquity into the 1500s, there is nonetheless a near-universal acceptance of dreaming as integral to the lives of individuals and communities. Only from the seventeenth century does this singular element of sleeping begin to be marginalized and discredited. Dreaming cannot be accommodated within conceptions of mental life based on empirical sense perception or on abstract rational thought. Even earlier, by the mid

1400s, there is a rejection of the possibility of an interplay between dream and waking in European art with the development of representational techniques designed and quantified to exclude the illogic and inconsistencies of dream vision. Certainly, counter-systemic attitudes to sleep and dream persisted on the fringes of a modernizing West, although there was a vast dispossession and disempowerment in the eighteenth and nineteenth centuries, when dreaming was severed from any residual links to a magico-theological framework. The imaginative capability of the dreaming sleeper underwent a relentless erosion, and the vitiated identity of a visionary was left over for a tolerated minority of poets, artists, and mad people. Modernization could not proceed in a world populated with large numbers of individuals who believed in the value or potency of their own internal visions or voices.

Beginning in the nineteenth century, new industries of image-making (and later auditory formats) fundamentally transformed the very possibility of "visionary" experience. In the 1830s and 1840s, there was an increasing amount of research on the features of human vision considered to be "subjective," or belonging to the body as the result of internal causes or activity. The most significant category of these were retinal after-images, nervous and optical phenomena vividly discernible to the perceiver *with eyes closed*. An accumulation of scientific studies on the temporalities of after-images led quickly to the development of corresponding technologies through which perceptual experience could be produced externally for a new kind of visual consumer.[3] These included the phenakistiscope, the zoetrope, and later a variety of other pre-cinematic entertainments. However, a very different class of subjective visual events was also explored, beginning in the 1830s, often by the same researchers. Far more resistant to any quantification or mastery, these came to be known as hypna-gogic images: the multiform visual occurrences (often inseparable from other sense modalities) that are unique to a state of consciousness hovering between wakefulness and sleep. Yet knowledge of this evasive phenomenon plainly could not lead to any practical or commodifiable applications, and by the end of the nineteenth century the study of hypnagogic images had ceased, or was pursued mainly in work on patho-logical conditions, dissociative states, or personality disorders. As a postscript, nearly a century later, Italo Calvino remarked near the end of his life that civilization as a whole was on the verge of "losing a basic human faculty: the power of bringing visions into focus with our eyes shut."[4]

Perhaps the most consequential moment in the devaluation of dream occurred in the very last year of the nineteenth century, when Freud completed *The Interpretation of Dreams*. Here he famously designated dreaming as a cordoned-off arena of primi-tive irrationality: "What once dominated waking life while the mind was still young and incompetent seems now to have been banished into the night . . . Dreaming is a piece of infantile mental life that has been superseded."[5] In fact Freud was unset-tled by dreaming just as he was by trance states, and his work in this area is a Procrustean bed on which he attempted to domesti-cate what was outside his control or understanding. Even though we have been in the post-Freudian era for some time, reductive versions of his ideas have become common-sense assumptions for many who have never read a word of his work.

The widely held truism that all dreaming is the scrambled, disguised expression of a repressed wish is a colossal reduction of the multiplicity of dream experiences. The readiness of much of Western culture to accept the general outlines of such a thesis is merely evidence of the thoroughness with which the primacy of individual desire and want had penetrated and shaped bourgeois self-understandings by the early twentieth century. As Ernst Bloch and others have argued, the nature of wishes and drives has gone through enormous historical changes over the last 400 years.[6] This is not even to address a much longer time frame during which the notion of "individual desires" may have been meaningless. Over a century later, it is not difficult to see the irrelevance of some of Freud's proposals. It is impossible now to conjure up an *individual* wish or desire so unavowable that it cannot be consciously acknowledged and vicariously gratified. Now, during waking hours, reality shows and websites indifferently detail every conceivable "prohibited" family romance or antagonism, while web pornography and violent gaming cater to any previously unmentionable desire. The unavowable now, in this milieu, is any wish for a collective overturning of omnipresent conditions of social isolation, economic injustice, and compulsory self-interestedness.

But Freud's privatization of dreams is only one sign of a broader erasure of the possibility of their trans-individualistic significance. Throughout the twentieth century, it was generally unthinkable that wishes could be for anything other than *individual* needs—wishes for a dream house, a dream car, or a vacation. Freud was one of many for whom the group or community played only a regressive part in an economy of desire, and his work is merely one instance of a bourgeois horror of the crowd, or the horde, whose group actions were inevitably unthinking and infantile repudiations of mature individual responsibility. But the psychoanalytic reduction not only prohibits wishes and needs that transcend individual desire and acquisitiveness; it also refuses the possibility of dreaming as a ceaseless and turbulent convergence of the lived present with ghosts from a fugitive and still indiscernable future. It categorically binds all dreaming, all wishes, within a closed field of forgotten events in the earliest years of one's life, and disempowers the dreamer further by restricting the ability to understand them to the analyst. Dreams may well be the vehicles of wishes, but the wishes at stake are the insatiable human desires to exceed the isolating and privatizing confines of the self.

Of the few voices in the twentieth century to make claims for the social importance of dream, one of the best known was André Breton, supported by his peers, like Desnos, in the Surrealist group. Stimulated by Freud's work but aware of its limits, Breton outlined a creative reciprocity or circulation between waking events and dreams that would be part of a revolution on the terrain of the everyday life. His intention was to break down any opposition between action and dreaming, and to affirm that one would nourish the other. But in the early

1930s, when Breton was writing, these proposals collided with prevailing leftist assumptions in which a commitment to revolutionary praxis seemed the antithesis of dreaming as merely an impotent wish for change. The subsequent course of events in Europe in the 1930s obviously made it more difficult for Breton's proposals to seem politically relevant. Nonetheless, his pages in *Les vases communicants*, in which he imagines Paris being viewed at the breaking of dawn from the hilltop of the Sacré-Coeur, are an extraordinary evocation of the latent desires and collective powers of a multitude of sleepers.[7] He conjures up in the liminal moment between darkness and light, between the restoration of sleep and the working day, a collaboration yet to come between work and dreams that will animate "the sweeping away of the capitalist world." Little wonder that Freud responded to this text, sent to him by Breton, with patronizing incomprehension.

But at least psychoanalysis took a serious if narrow interest in dreaming, positioning it as a state that could indirectly provide knowledge of processes inaccessible to empirical investigation (at least before the new tools of the neurosciences). Far more prevalent today is the indifferent dismissal of dreams as a mere self-regulatory adjustment of the sensory overload of waking life. The specific content of the dream, whether semantic or affective, is essentially irrelevant to neurochemical explanations. With the exception of new-age books and therapies centered around dreaming as a path to "inner growth" or self-understanding, most people remain incognizant of and uninterested in their own periodic dream production, which might superficially seem like a series of pitifully drab or deficient versions of mass-media productions of what purport to be dreams.

We are now in an era in which there is an overarching prohibition on wishes other than those linked to individual acquisition, accumulation, and power. In a 24/7 world these limits are as much self-enforced as they are imposed externally, but the possibility of self-regulation is the result of developments reaching back many decades. As much as it targeted the kind of social compromises associated with the New Deal, neoliberalism also required the dismantling and effacing of the concrete political and social achievements of the 1960s. An array of hopes, ideas, and practices associated retrospectively with the cultures of the 1960s in the US and parts of Europe had to be extirpated or discredited. As Immanuel Wallerstein and others have convincingly argued, it is erroneous to depict 1968 as anything other than the crest of a world revolution, unprecedented in scale, consisting of plural struggles in many sites with complex determinations. Similarly, the last thirty years or more have to be understood as a long phase of sustained counter-revolution. Obviously, the magnitude of the anti-systemic insurrections in Asia, Latin America, and the urban ghettos of the US demanded the massive use of interconnected forms of economic, penal, and military violence over this period—forms of violence that continue to evolve in the present, as a new wave of struggles and "springtimes" has begun to coalesce. For example, the current mass incarceration of millions of

111

African-Americans has its origins in the aftermath of the urban uprisings of the 1960s.

But a parallel counter-insurgency, taking shape in the late 1970s, was primarily ideological, although sweeping in scope. Its target was a tentative constellation of forms of sociality that needed to be destroyed or deformed to produce acquiescence in the face of the global shift to harsher forms of finance capital and the expanding monetization of everyday life. Intertwined with the specifically political movements of the 1960s were a wide range of informal challenges to institutional demands for privatization, social separation, the acquisitiveness of consumerism, and the maintenance of class hierarchies. They were challenges that took place often stammeringly, naively, incompletely—through the actions and inventiveness of new collectivities and subjectivities, but also through the defense of existing communities. These included the transient occupation and activation of social spaces, the claiming of de-individualized notions of the body and the self, experiments with language and alternate forms of exchange, the creation of new sexualities, and the sustaining of marginalities defined not by a repressive center but by their own shifting modes of organization.

Of the many layers of 1960s culture and politics, several pervasive and interrelated phenomena required sustained counter-action and obliteration over the long term. Foremost, perhaps, was the collective and individual understanding, arrived at in the 1960s through direct experiences, that happiness could be unrelated to ownership, to acquiring products, or to individual status, and could instead emerge directly out of the shared life and action of groups. Gary Snyder's words from 1969 represent one of many articulations of this pervasive if short-lived ethos: "True affluence is not needing any *thing.*" Equally threatening to power were new forms of association that introduced at least a limited permeability of social class and a range of affronts to the sanctity of private property. The chimerical inducements and promises of upward mobility began to lose their effectiveness on young people, and there were pervasive if diffuse challenges to the centrality and necessity of work. "Dropping out" was more fundamentally disturbing on a systemic level than many are prepared to admit. The 1980s saw the start of a sustained campaign to turn material poverty into something shameful and repellent. The anti-war movement had spawned both a broad identification with pacifism and public empathy for the victims of war; but in the 1980s the conditions nurturing these currents had to be eliminated and replaced in all areas with a culture of aggressivity and violence. That millions of supposedly liberal or progressive Americans now will dutifully avow that they "support our troops" while remaining silent about the thousands murdered in imperial wars attests to the success of these counter-measures. Beginning in the 1980s and continuing since, these events of the 1960s and their participants have been ferociously converted into hollow caricatures, into objects of ridicule, demonization, and trivialization. But the extensiveness and malevolence of the historical falsifications are an index of the danger levels the culture of the 1960s posed, even in its afterlife. Though the experimentation of the period with communitarian forms may have seemed new in relation to the left of the 1930s and 1940s, it was partly a resurfacing of the half-buried dreams of the nineteenth century, when the possibility of a socialism of mutual support, of a world divested of private property, flourished as visible elements of a contested collective imagination.

The main thrust of the counter-revolution has been either the elimination or the financialization of social arrangements that had previously supported many kinds of cooperative activity. Through the appropriation of public spaces and resources into the logic of the marketplace, individuals are dispossessed of many collective forms of mutual support or sharing. A simple and pervasive cooperative practice like hitchhiking had to be inverted into a risk-filled act with fearful, even lethal consequences. Now it has reached the point of laws being enacted in parts of the United States that criminalize giving food to the homeless or to undocumented immigrants.

Fredric Jameson and others have detailed the operation of a cultural prohibition, at the structural level, on even the imagining of alternatives to the desolate insularity of individual experience within the competitive workings of capitalist society. Possibilities of non-monadic or communal life are rendered unthinkable. In 1965, a typical negative image of collective living was, for example, that of the Bolsheviks moving sullen working-class families into Doctor Zhivago's spacious and pristine home in the David Lean movie. For the past quarter-century, the communal has been presented as a far more nightmarish option. For example, in recent neoconservative portrayals of the

Chinese Cultural Revolution, measures taken against private property and class privilege on behalf of collective social formations are equated to the most monstrous crimes in world history. On a smaller scale, there are the countless narratives of cult-like communes of obedient converts ruled by homicidal madmen and cynical manipulators. Echoing bourgeois fears in the late nineteenth century following 1871, the idea of a commune derived from any form of socialism remains systemically intolerable. The cooperative, as a lived set of relations, cannot actually be made visible—it can only be represented as a parodic replication of existing relations of domination. In many different ways, the attack on values of collectivity and cooperation is articulated through the notion that freedom is to be free of any dependence on others, while in fact we are experiencing a more comprehensive subjection to the "free" workings of markets. As Harold Bloom has shown, the real American religion is "to be free of other selves." In academic circles, the right-wing attack on the cooperative is abetted by the current intellectual fashion of denouncing the idea or possibility of community for its alleged exclusions and latent fascisms. One of the main forms of control over the last thirty years has been to ensure there are no visible alternatives to privatized patterns of living.

Jean-Paul Sartre's *Critique of Dialectical Reason*, one of the great works of social thought from the 1960s, provided a powerful account of how a monadic life-world is perpetuated and rendered invisible. Yet this book, disparaged or ignored during the North American heyday of deconstruction in the Reagan-Thatcher era, has a remarkable relevance to the transformed textures of the contemporary everyday. Central to the *Critique* is its meditation on the systemic strategies of separation that prevent the objective reality of daily life from being perceived by the individuals who inhabit it—a problem no less acute today than when it was written, in the late 1950s. Among its many interrelated themes, it addressed our relative incapacity to see the nature of our own situatedness in the world. For better or worse, Sartre made the decision to use the somewhat ponderous term "practico-inert" as a crucial category of social reality. Yet the awkwardness of this neologism conveys something of the paradox of public and private life humming with an unimaginable quantity of activity, while all this restless animation and industry is in the service of an effective stasis, of maintaining the inertia of existing relations.

The practico-inert was thus Sartre's way of designating the sedimented, institutional everyday world constituted out of human energy but manifested as the immense accumulation of routine passive activity. It operates as a collective delusion that transforms the experience of individual solitude and powerlessness into something seemingly natural or inevitable. "The practico-inert field is the field of our servitude . . . to mechanical forces, and to anti-social apparatuses." His key term for this powerlessness is "seriality," and with it he provides his monumental account of the continuous production of loneliness as a fundamental underpinning of capitalism. Seriality is the dispersal of collectivity into an aggregate of discrete individuals who relate to each other only on the basis of hollow or narcissistic identities. To Sartre's celebrated examples of standing in line to board a bus, being stuck in traffic, and shopping at the super-market could be added the unfathomable amounts of human time expended today in desultory electronic activity and exchanges. Whether in the mid twentieth century or today, seriality is the numbing and ceaseless production of the same. It is the weight of all the counterfinalities that inexorably act against our own intentions, our loves and hopes.

Not by accident, Sartre—along with many other European critics—relied on Lewis Mumford's *Technics and Civilization*, a historical survey of rationalized forms of social organization that were dependent on an automation of behavior, on the training of humans to function habitually and repetitively. Sartre describes not only individual isolation but the seriality that underlies situations with a manifestly collective or group character. He uses the notion of "recurrence" to explain how forms of mass conformity and homogeneity are produced in consciousness or material culture. His extraordinary analysis of radio provides a model vitally relevant to recent debates about the consequences of telecommunications and social networks. Radio was an instance of what he termed "indirect gatherings," and it produced "a unity of individuals outside themselves but also determines them in separation and, in so far as they are separate, ensures their communication through alterity."[8] It is regrettable that his plan for a study of television in Volume 2 of the *Critique* was never fulfilled, although his notes for this section survive.

Sartre's project of historical understanding converges on a very different kind of group, in his theorization of the "fused group" or "group in fusion." It is only through this privileged but precarious formation that there is ever a possible route out of the nightmare of serialization and isolation. Its appearance in history means the realization of a group whose praxis has the capacity to create new forms of sociality, and many sections of the *Critique* are devoted to long analyses of the emergence of fused groups in particular revolutionary and anticolonial struggles. Deleuze and Guattari found Sartre's model to be "profoundly correct."[9] They saw it as an overturning of received ideas on class struggle: for Sartre there was no such thing as class spontaneity, only the spontaneity of the group. To be simply a member of a class or a political party was to remain locked in a serial identity. It was only a *perceptual* act—a non-habitual mode of looking—that could trigger an overcoming of the practico-inert, by the illuminating recognition of one's immediate and lived membership in a group of individuals with the same material and subjective experiences. To summarize broadly, it was to discern, in a moment charged with embitteredness or anger, a condition of commonality and interdependence. One made a leap of consciousness to apprehend one's own estrangement in others, and this discovery would be the basis for "the liquidation of seriality" and its "replacement by community." It was a revisualization of reality to include the understanding that there are shared goals and projects, that what one wants most can never be achieved individually, but only by the common praxis of a group, even if the group or community thus formed is historically impermanent.

In obvious ways, this section of the *Critique* raises crucial questions regarding the nature or possibility of revolutionary movements today, and about how groups actually come together. It also poses the question of whether current forms of electronic separation and perceptual management are part of conditions that would inhibit or deflect the processes Sartre details. In what ways are new strata of communication networks and their myriad applications essentially new strata of the practico-inert, new appropriations of daily life in which seriality is intrinsic to its mutating make-up? All the 24/7 electronic interfacing, all the mass immersion at a micrological level in contemporary technological culture, might easily be said to constitute a new negative unity of passivity and alterity.

Another very different book from the 1960s engaged some of these issues in ways also relevant to recent political events. In spite of the sectarian enmities of that time, it would be futile to claim that Debord's *Society of the Spectacle* (1967) was not marked by some of Sartre's formulations in the *Critique*. Of course, in place of the determinations of the group-in-fusion, Debord pursues the historical fate of workers' councils. However, the immediately vital questions addressed by both authors concern what circumstances either impede or enhance the possibilities of collective political action. It is of particular urgency given the continuation or aftermath of the insurrectionary events that began in 2011 in Tunisia, Egypt, Wisconsin, Spain, Oakland, Bahrain, Zuccotti Park, and elsewhere. It is worth remembering the concluding paragraphs of Debord's book, in which the problem of communication is foregrounded. He is hardly alone in emphasizing the link between the words "community" and "communication," where communication is not the transmission of messages but in some way an ethos of sharing. Spectacle, he writes, is the expropriation of that possibility; it is the production of a one-way communication that he characterizes as "a generalized autism." Debord saw that by the 1960s capitalism had produced a systematic breakdown in the faculty of encounter (*rencontre*), and "the replacement of that faculty by a social hallucination, an illusion of encounter."[10]

The contemporary relevance of these texts, especially at a time when extravagant and dubious claims are advanced on behalf of the revolutionary potential of social media, is that they enable us to ask what kinds of encounter are in fact possible today. More specifically, what are the encounters that can lead to new formations, to new insurgent capabilities, and where can they take place—in what spaces or temporalities? How much of the exchange and circulation of information occurring electronically today is a colossal amplification of what Sartre termed "an inversion of praxis into practico-inert activity"? How much of the blogging transpiring globally—on the part of individuals numbering in the hundreds of millions, often using the language of resistance—is equivalent to the mass autism that Debord noted? Obviously, political activism means creatively using available tools and material resources, but it should not entail imagining the tools themselves to have intrinsic redemptive values. Lenin, Trotsky, and their cohort made use of every communications technology at hand in 1917, but they never elevated them to privileged and sacrosanct determinants of an entire constellation of historical events, as some cyberactivists have done in extolling the role of social media in recent political movements and uprisings. Once there is mystification and the attribution of quasi-magical capabilities to networks, it becomes like faith in a Ponzi scheme that will automatically pay off on behalf of the weak and oppressed. The myths of the egalitarian and empowering nature of this technology have been cultivated for a reason. Police agencies of the global order can only be gratified by the willingness of activists to concentrate their organizing around internet strategies, by which they voluntarily kettle themselves in cyberspace, where state surveillance, sabotage, and manipulation are far easier than in lived communities and localities where actual encounters occur. If one's goal is radical social transformation, electronic media in their current forms of mass availability are not useless—but only when they are subordinate to struggles and encounters taking place elsewhere. If networks are not in the service of already existing relationships forged out of shared experience and proximity, they will always reproduce and reinforce the separations, the opacity, the dissimulations, and the self-interestedness inherent in their use. Any social turbulence whose primary sources are in the use of social media will inevitably be historically ephemeral and inconsequential.

Chantal Akerman's film *D'Est* (*From the East*), made in 1992 and early 1993, carries a heightened self-consciousness about the circumstances of this weighty historical moment. Shot mainly in Poland and Russia in the year and a half following the dissolution of the Soviet Union, it discloses a world in suspension, on the edge of an undetermined future, yet still weighed down by long-standing patterns and habits. Using very long takes, it is an extended portrayal of certain textures of everyday life, sometimes suggesting a Sartrean seriality. In her essay on *D'Est*, Akerman famously declared that she felt the need to make the film "while there's still time" ("tant qu'il en est encore temps").[11] In one sense, she meant that she had to finish the project before it was too late, before cultural and economic forces transformed the subject of her work into something different, even unrecognizable. But, given the choices she made of what to record, "while there's still time" is also a way of saying: while there is still a world of time-in-common, a world sustained by a collective inhabiting and sharing of time and its rhythms, in the older sense of the word "quotidian."

Like many in the early 1990s, Akerman understood that the collapse of the Soviet Union and its hold on eastern Europe would facilitate the final globalization of the West and the implantation everywhere of its values and demands. Thus her film was made with an awareness of the fleeting interregnum it documented. Akerman realizes that the oppositions supposedly sustaining the bipolar Cold War world had become mostly illusory, but nonetheless she affirms that "the east" in her film retained singular and long-standing cultural forms that were on the brink of being obliterated by the expansion of Western capitalism. Even though Akerman cautions against any simplistic logic of before and after, *D'Est* is the testament of a social world, however damaged, prior to the imposition of neoliberal financialization, privatization, and social atomization. It is a film about living in a milieu where "there is still time," before the 24/7 non-time of compulsory accumulation, of individual choice.

D'Est records journeys across territory, through seasonal time, from summer to winter. In ways that recall Arendt, the film also moves between crowded, collectively occupied public spaces and the very different textures of sheltered domestic spaces. But, more than anything else, *D'Est* conveys the time of waiting. It does this most compellingly in its extended tracking shots of people standing in line or waiting in railroad stations. Akerman shows the act of waiting for itself, without a goal, never disclosing why a crowd is formed into a line. As Sartre showed, the queue is one of the many banal instances in which the conflict between the individual and the organization of society is felt, but at the level of the unthought or unseen. Certainly, Akerman lets us see the queue as Sartre did, as a plurality of separations that become "the negation of reciprocity." But one of her revelatory achievements is also to show the act of waiting as something essential to the experience of being together, to the tentative possibility of community. It is a time in which encounters can occur. Mixed in with the annoyances and frustrations is the humble and artless dignity of waiting, of being patient as deference to others, as a tacit acceptance of time shared in common. The suspended, unproductive time of waiting, of taking turns, is inseparable from any form of cooperation or mutuality. All the preceding decades of authoritarian rule had not eradicated certain enduring features of community, in part because the brutal but crude forms of Stalinist discipline allowed many of the underlying rhythms of social time to persist unchanged.

The forms of control accompanying the rise of neoliberalism in the 1990s were more invasive in their subjective effects and in their devastation of shared and collectively supported relations. 24/7 presents the delusion of a time without waiting, of an on-demand instantaneity, of having and getting insulated from the presence of others. The responsibility for other people that proximity entails can now easily be bypassed by the electronic management of one's daily routines and contacts. Perhaps more importantly, 24/7 has produced an atrophy of the individual patience and deference that are essential to any form of direct democracy: the patience to listen to others, to wait one's turn to speak. The phenomenon of blogging is one example—among many—of the triumph of a one-way model of auto-chattering in which the possibility of ever having to wait and listen to someone else has been eliminated. Blogging, no matter what its intentions, is thus one of the many announcements of the end of politics. The waiting that one actually does now—in traffic jams or airport lines—acts to intensify resentment and competitiveness with those nearby. One of the superficial but piercing truisms about class society is that the rich never have to wait, and this feeds the desire to emulate wherever possible this particular privilege of the elite.

The problem of waiting is tied to the larger issue of the

incompatibility of 24/7 capitalism with any social behaviors that have a rhythmic pattern of action and pause. This would include any social exchange involving sharing, reciprocity, or cooperation. Underlying all of these is the model of "taking turns," requiring alternating states of assertiveness and acquiescence. In the 1920s, the social philosopher George Herbert Mead attempted to name the constitutive elements of human society—those without which society as such would not be possible. For Mead, these are neighborliness, helpfulness, and cooperation. "The fundamental attitude of helping the other person who is down, who finds himself in sickness or other misfortune, belongs to the very structure of individuals in a human community."[12] Mead also insists that, for thousands of years, these values were also the basis of economic exchange: "There is a participation in the attitude of need, each putting himself in the attitude of the other in the recognition of the mutual value which the exchange has for both." Mead's work can be faulted for its pervasive ahistoricism, but here his universalizing of the cooperative core of a social world brings into view more clearly the discordance between twenty-first-century capitalism and society itself. It also provides a background relevant for Bernard Stiegler's diagnosis of a contemporary global pathology that renders care for others or oneself impossible.

As I indicated earlier, sleep is one of the few remaining experiences where, knowingly or not, we abandon ourselves to the care of others. As solitary and private as sleep may seem, it is not yet severed from an interhuman tracery of mutual support and trust, however damaged many of these links may be. It is also a periodic release from individuation—a nightly unraveling of the loosely woven tangle of the shallow subjectivities one inhabits and manages by day. In the depersonalization of slumber, the sleeper inhabits a world in common, a shared enactment of withdrawal from the calamitous nullity and waste of 24/7 praxis. However, for all the ways in which sleep is unexploitable and unassimilable, it is hardly an enclave outside the existing global order. Sleep has always been porous, suffused with the flows of waking activity, though today it is more unshielded than ever from assaults that corrode and diminish it. In spite of these degradations, sleep is the recurrence in our lives of a waiting, of a pause. It affirms the necessity of postponement, and the deferred retrieval or recommencement of whatever has been postponed. Sleep is a remission, a release from the "constant continuity" of all the threads in which one is enmeshed while waking. It seems too obvious to state that sleep requires periodic disengagement from networks and devices in order to enter a state of inactivity and uselessness. It is a form of time that leads us elsewhere than to the things we own or are told we need.

In my account, modern sleep includes the interval before sleep—the lying awake in quasi-darkness, waiting indefinitely for the desired loss of consciousness. During this suspended time, there is a recovery of perceptual capacities that are disabled or disregarded during the day. Involuntarily, one reclaims a sensitivity or responsiveness to both internal and external sensations within a non-metric duration. One hears sounds of traffic, a dog barking, the hum of a white-noise machine, police sirens, heat pipes clanking, or feels the quick twitching of one's limbs, the pounding of blood in one's temples, and sees the granular fluctuations of retinal luminosity with one's eyes shut. One follows an uneven succession of groundless points of temporary focus and shifting alertness, as well as the wavering onset of hypnagogic events. Sleep coincides with the metabolizing of what is ingested by day: drugs, alcohol, all the detritus from interfacing with illuminated screens; but also the flood of anxieties, fears, doubts, longings, imaginings of failure or the big score. This is the monotony of sleep and sleeplessness, night after night. In its repetition and unconcealment, it is one of the unvanquishable remnants of the everyday.

One of the many reasons human cultures have long associated sleep with death is that they each demonstrate the continuity of the world in our absence. However, the only temporary absence of the sleeper always contains a bond to a future, to a possibility of renewal and hence of freedom. It is an interval into which glimpses of an unlived life, of a postponed life, can edge faintly into awareness. The nightly hope for the insensible state of deep sleep is at the same time an anticipation of an awakening that could hold something unforeseen. In Europe after 1815, during several decades of counter-revolution, reversals, and derailments of hope, there were artists and poets who intuited that sleep was not necessarily an evasion or escape from history. Shelley and Courbet, for example, are two who understood that sleep was another form of historical time—that its withdrawal and apparent passivity also encompassed the unrest and inquietude of becoming that was essential to the nascence of a more just and egalitarian future. Now, in the twenty-first century, the disquiet of sleep has a more troubling relation to the future. Located somewhere on the border between the social and the natural, sleep ensures the presence in the world of the phasic and cyclical patterns essential to life and incompatible with capitalism. Sleep's anomalous persistence has to be understood in relation to the ongoing destruction of the processes that sustain existence on the planet. Because capitalism cannot limit itself, the notion of preservation or conservation is a systemic impossibility. Against this background, the restorative inertness of sleep counters the deathliness of all the accumulation, financialization, and waste that have devastated anything once held in common. Now there is actually only one dream, superseding all others: it is of a shared world whose fate is not terminal, a world without billionaires, which has a future other than barbarism or the post-human, and in which history can take on other forms than reified nightmares of catastrophe. It is possible that—in many different places, in many disparate states, including reverie or daydream—the imaginings of a future without capitalism begin as dreams of sleep. These would be intimations of sleep as a radical interruption, as a refusal of the unsparing weight of our global present, of sleep which, at the most mundane level of everyday experience, can always rehearse the outlines of what more consequential renewals and beginnings might be.

ENDNOTES

Chapter One

1 The Defense Advanced Research Projects Agency.
2 Jane Mayer, *The Dark Side*, New York: Doubleday, 2008, p. 206.
3 Teresa Brennan, *Globalization and Its Terrors: Daily Life in the West*, London: Routledge, 2003, pp. 19–22.
4 Luc Boltanski and Eve Chiapello, *The New Spirit of Capitalism*, London: Verso, p. 155.
5 Wolfgang Schivelbusch, *Disenchanted Night: The Industrialization of Light in the Nineteenth Century*, transl. Angela Davies, Berkeley, CA: University of California Press, 1988.
6 Maurice Blanchot, *The Writing of the Disaster*, transl. Ann Smock, Lincoln, NE: University of Nebraska Press, 1995, pp. 48–50.

7   For some of Levinas's many discussions of insomnia, see *Existence and Existents*, transl. A. Lingis, Pittsburgh: Duquesne University Press, 2001; and *Otherwise than Being*, transl. A. Lingis, Pittsburgh: Duquesne University Press, 1998.

8   See, for example, Jean-Luc Nancy, *The Inoperative Community*, Minneapolis: University of Minnesota Press, 1991.

9   Hannah Arendt, *The Human Condition*, Chicago: University of Chicago, 1958, p. 134.

10 Friedrich Nietzsche, *Twilight of the Idols*, transl. R. J. Hollingdale, London: Penguin, 1968, p. 33.

11 Roland Barthes, *The Neutral*, transl. Rosalind E. Krauss and Denis Hollier, New York: Columbia University Press, 2005, p. 37.

Chapter Two

1   Gilles Deleuze and Félix Guattari, A *Thousand Plateaus*, transl. Brian Massumi, Minneapolis: University of Minnesota Press, 1987, pp. 107–9.

2   Giorgio Agamben, *What Is an Apparatus?* transl. David Kishik and Stefan Pedatella, Palo Alto, CA: Stanford University Press, 2009, p. 21.

3   Fredric Jameson, Lecture at Film Society of Lincoln Center, New York, June 12, 2011.

4   See Bernard Stiegler, *De la misère symbolique Vol. 1: L'époque hyperindustrielle*, Paris: Galilée, 2004.

5 Bernard Stiegler, *Acting Out*, transl. Patrick Crogan, Palo Alto, CA: Stanford University Press, 2009, pp. 39–59.

6 Paul Valéry, "Remarks on Intelligence," in *Collected Works of Paul Valéry*, vol. 10, transl. Denise Folliot and Jackson Mathews, Bollingen Series, Princeton, NJ: Princeton University Press, 1962, pp. 80–3.

7 See Tiqqun, *Théorie du Bloom*, La Fabrique: Paris, 2004.

Chapter Three

1 Andrew Ure, *The Philosophy of Manufactures* (1835), cited in Karl Marx, *The Poverty of Philosophy*, New York: International Publishers, 1963, p. 141. Marx quotes this same passage from Ure in *Capital*, vol. 1.

2 Karl Marx, *Grundrisse*, transl. Martin Nicolaus, London: Vintage, 1973, p. 669.

3 Ibid., p. 524.

4 Fredric Jameson, "The End of Temporality," *Critical Inquiry*, Summer 2003, p. 699.

5 Richard Overy, *Why the Allies Won*, London: Norton, 1995, p. 5.

6 Gilles Deleuze, "Postscript on Control Societies," in *Negotiations*, transl. Martin Joughin, New York: Columbia University Press, 1995, pp. 177–82.

7 See Zygmunt Bauman, *Liquid Modernity*, Cambridge, UK: Polity, 2000, pp. 53–76.

8 Guy Debord, *Comments on the Society of the Spectacle*, transl. Malcolm Imrie, London: Verso, 1990, p. 10.

9   See Christa Degnan, "Novell's Schmidt Outlines 'Digital Me' Technology," *PC Week Online*, March 22, 1999.

10 John Dewey, *Experience and Nature*, Chicago: Open Court, 1925, p. 229.

11 On the competing institutional models of television in the 1930s, see my "Attention, Spectacle, Counter-Memory," in Tom McDonough, ed., *Guy Debord and the Situationist International*, Cambridge, MA: MIT Press, 2002.

12 Michael Waldman, Sean Nicholson, and Nodir Adilov, "Does Television Cause Autism?" NBER Working Paper Series, No. 12632 (2006).

13 Raymond Williams, *Television: Technology and Cultural Form*, New York: Schocken, 1974.

14 Robert Kubey and Mihaly Csikszentmihalyi, *Television and the Quality of Life: How Viewing Shapes Everyday Experience*, Abingdon, UK: Erlbaum, 1990.

Chapter Four

1   Laura Mulvey, *Death 24x a Second*, London: Reaktion, 2006, pp. 87–8.

2   See Stephen Bann, *The Clothing of Clio*, Cambridge, UK: Cambridge University Press, 1984.

3   See my *Techniques of the Observer*, Cambridge, MA: MIT Press, 1991.

4   Italo Calvino, *Six Memos for the Next Millenium*, Cambridge, MA: Harvard University Press, 1988, p. 92.

5 Sigmund Freud, *The Interpretation of Dreams*, transl. James Strachey, New York, Avon, 1965, p. 606.

6 Ernst Bloch, *The Principle of Hope*, vol. 1, Cambridge, MA: MIT Press, 1986, pp. 49–50.

7 André Breton, *Communicating Vessels*, transl. Mary Ann Caws and Geoffrey T. Harris, Lincoln, NE: University of Nebraska Press, 1990 (1932).

8 Jean-Paul Sartre, *Critique of Dialectical Reason*, vol. 1, transl. Alan Sheridan-Smith, London: Verso, 1976, p. 271.

9 Gilles Deleuze and Félix Guattari, *Anti-Oedipus*, transl. Mark Seem, New York: Viking, 1977, p. 256.

10 Guy Debord, *The Society of the Spectacle*, transl. Donald Nicholson-Smith, New York: Zone Books, 1995, pp. 152–3.

11 Chantal Akerman, "On *D'Est*," in *Bordering on Fiction: Chantal Akerman's D'Est*, Minneapolis: Walker Art Center, 1995, p. 17.

12 George Herbert Mead, *Mind, Self and Society*, ed. Charles Morris, Chicago: University of Chicago Press, 1934, p. 258.